AUSTRALIAN ARMY COMBAT SUPPORT SERIES – 1

GALL

AN AUSTRALIAN MEDICAL PERSPECTIVE

Michael Tyquin

ARMY·HISTORY·UNIT

PROTECTING ARMY HERITAGE
PROMOTING ARMY HISTORY

© Copyright Army History Unit
Campbell Park Offices (CP2-5-166)
Canberra ACT 2600
AUSTRALIA
(02) 6266 4248
(02) 6266 4044 – fax
Copyright 2012 © Commonwealth of Australia

First published 2012

All inquiries should be made to the publishers.

Big Sky Publishing Pty Ltd
PO Box 303, Newport, NSW 2106, Australia
Phone: 1300 364 611
Fax: (61 2) 9918 2396
Email: info@bigskypublishing.com.au
Web: www.bigskypublishing.com.au

National Library of Australia Cataloguing-in-Publication entry (pbk)

Author: Tyquin, Michael B. (Michael Bernard), 1952-

Title: Gallipoli : an Australian medical perspective / Michael Tyquin.

ISBN: 9781921941863 (pbk.)

Notes: Includes bibliographical references and index.

Subjects: Australia. Army. Medical Corps--History.
        Medicine, Military--Australia--History.
        War--Medical aspects.
        World War, 1914-1918--Medical care--Australia.
        World War, 1914-1918--Campaigns--Turkey--Gallipoli
        Peninsula--Participation, Australian.

Dewey Number: 940.5475

National Library of Australia Cataloguing-in-Publication entry (ebook)

Author: Tyquin, Michael B. (Michael Bernard), 1952-

Title: Gallipoli [electronic resource]: an Australian medical perspective / Michael Tyquin.

ISBN: 9781921941870 (ebook)

Notes: Includes bibliographical references and index.

Subjects: Australia. Army. Medical Corps--History.
        Medicine, Military--Australia--History.
        War--Medical aspects.
        World War, 1914-1918--Medical care--Australia.
        World War, 1914-1918--Campaigns--Turkey--Gallipoli
        Peninsula--Participation, Australian.

Dewey Number: 940.5475

Cover design and typesetting by Think Productions, Melbourne

Front cover and title page: View of Rest Gully, showing dugouts on the side of the hill, the 5th Australian Field Ambulance. AWM A01869.
Back cover: Main - 2nd Australian Field Ambulance practising boat drill in the harbour on the Aegean island of Lemnos in preparation for the landing at Anzac Cove. AWM C01632. Top - Stretcher Bearer AWM A01522. Mid - Red Cross sash AWM REL34450_10001. Bottom - Horse drawn Ambulance AWM J02139.

Printed in China through Bookbuilders.

Contents

Australian Army Combat Support Series

In 2004 the then Chief of Army Advisory Group, comprising the Army's senior generals, established a scheme to promote the study and understanding of military history in the Army. From this decision the *Campaign Series* was established, with its focus on Army's future leaders.

The success of the *Campaign Series* identified the need to document and analyse other aspects of our military history that are not specifically a battle or campaign, or that approaches an element of military service or explores military materiel in support of operations. The *Australian Army Combat Support Series* was established for this purpose. As with the *Campaign Series* the *Australian Army Combat Support Series* will include extensive visual information including specifically prepared maps in colour and 3D, commissioned artwork, photographs and computer graphics.

The *Australian Army Combat Support Series* complements Army's other history publications, which produce academically rigorous and referenced analytical works. The Australian Army History Unit sees this series growing into another significant contribution to the history of the Australian Army, one that will provide an excellent introduction to Australia's Military History.

Roger Lee, Army Historian

Acknowledgments

I would like to thank my long-time colleague and sometime chief Roger Lee, head of the Army History Unit, who is responsible for resurrecting this work in a different guise for a new audience. I remain in debt to the staff at the Australian War Memorial, the National Library of Australia, and the state libraries of Victoria and New South Wales. This book would not have been possible without the assistance of many individuals in various archives in London. These include the National Archives (formerly the Public Records Office, Kew), the Wellcome Institute, the Imperial War Museum, Kings College, and the Caird Library of the National Maritime Museum, Greenwich.

This work has been considerably enhanced by the generously offered skills of John Donovan (editing), Mark Walhert (maps), Jeff Isaacs (illustrations) and suggestions by Glenn Wahlert. I was able also to make use of several photographs courtesy of the Wellcome Trust and the Science Museum in London. Mr. Denny Neave was an understanding publisher bringing this book to print.

Preface

Much of this book is an updating and re-assessment of my 1993 work, Gallipoli: the Medical War. What follows has been written in a different style for a largely military audience; it takes advantage of more recent scholarship on the campaign, especially from Turkish sources, which contribute to our current understanding of the Gallipoli campaign.

To be successful, a modern army needs logistical support to survive - to arm, feed, transport, and care for its soldiers. The maintenance of health in any army, as history shows us, is a key factor in warfare.

When Australia entered the 1914-1918 War (World War I), the Army Medical Services (AMS) had only recently been brought together after the federation of the Australian colonies in 1901. Like the rest of the 1st Australian Imperial Force (AIF), the AMS was largely an untested organisation of volunteers based on a small cadre of professionals. The prime function of the AMS was to maintain healthy troops at the front or during operations, and to return the sick and injured to duty as soon as possible.

In many respects the Gallipoli campaign was a doomed undertaking, whose sad end has helped to shape our national identity. The seeds of ultimate defeat in December 1915 were the risks that attended a hugely ambitious, complex, and large-scale amphibious operation - the landings on well-defended shores on the Gallipoli peninsula, under cover of darkness. Communications at the time were primitive, while general staff officers had little understanding of the limitations or needs of the medical organisation, and their own medical assets.

Many Australians are still unaware that the Ottoman forces facing our troops were not only well prepared, but fully expected a landing somewhere along the Gallipoli peninsula. It is no surprise, therefore, that the whole force was very nearly evacuated a few days later.

It is important to remember that this was only one small episode in the much bigger story that was World War I. Gallipoli's successes and failures must be considered in that light. Despite the undoubted bravery of the Diggers, they did not fight in a vacuum. Their opponents were the Askers or Mehmetçiks (the Turkish equivalent of Diggers) of the Ottoman army.

Our allies, who shared many of the same privations, came from the British, New Zealand, Indian, and French armies. The Australian Army Medical Corps (AAMC) received aid from, and gave support to, all five forces at various times during 1915. This aspect of what we would now recognise as coalition support worked well for most of the campaign.

April, August, and December 1915 have been chosen in this study as significant, because it was during those months that particular challenges and problems, which were not necessarily there during the entire campaign, presented themselves to the medical services. These problems centred on surges of large numbers of battle casualties, outbreaks of disease, and serious defects in the medical management and evacuation system.

Underlying the execution of the Dardanelles campaign were factors wholly outside the control of the Australian AMS. Undoubtedly tragic, and sometimes avoidable, errors were made at the highest level of command, with subsequent pressures on the AMS. An amphibious operation of this type and scale, however, was without parallel in modern military history, and mistakes were inevitable, as they are with any campaign of such complexity.

Australian infantry private. (Jeff Isaacs)

I have attempted also to explode some of the more popular myths: the 'surprise' element in the initial landing; the stereotype of the 'bronzed Anzac'; British responsibility for major mistakes; and the impeccable image of Australian officers and soldiers. By the 1920s some of these myths had not yet progressed into our national folklore, like the singular bravery of Private John Simpson (Kirkpatrick) and his donkey Murphy, while others, such as the poor quality of the Ottoman army, still persist.

Ottoman infantry private. (Jeff Isaacs)

Privates and non-commissioned officers (NCOs) working in field ambulances and stretcher-bearers (who were not members of the AAMC) are here designated 'medics', though this term was not in use during World War I.

Note on Terminology:

In this book, Australian formations are given their titles (1st Division, 3rd Brigade). Allied formations alongside which they fought are given a national designator (29th British Division, New Zealand Brigade, 26th Indian Mountain Battery). Ottoman unit and formation titles are in Italics, as are the names of all ships, of either side. Non-English terms are also in Italics.

CHAPTER 1:

Why Gallipoli?

The outstanding features of the Dardanelles campaign were the comparative shortness of its duration, the intensity of the struggle in a confined area, and the exceptionally large numbers of battle and non-battle casualties.1

Neither side was fully prepared for the Gallipoli campaign. Allied planning for the landings was not well coordinated, and the medical organisation for the campaign was poorly developed.

It is important to note also that the opposing Ottoman army was still rebuilding itself after catastrophic losses in the Balkan Wars of 1912 and 1913, conflicts that almost bankrupted the Ottoman Empire. On the eve of the landing, crippling logistics shortages and a primitive Lines of Communications system (the military term of the day) meant that mobilisation was painstakingly slow and inadequate. Ottoman troops on Gallipoli, however, were forewarned, well prepared, well officered, and experienced – a stark contrast to the profile of the invading force.

MEDICAL ORGANISATION

At the beginning of the war, the AAMC consisted of a very small permanent army staff whose functions were administration and training. In addition there were a Militia Army Medical Corps, a Volunteer Army Medical Corps, and an Army Nursing Service Reserve.

In July 1914 the official strength of the Corps in the permanent army establishment stood at only four officers, including the Director-General of Medical Services (DGMS), Surgeon-General William Williams (founder of the AAMC), and 29 Other Ranks (ORs). A further 183 Officers and 1649 ORs served in the militia. Naturally, its organisation was modelled on the British Royal Army Medical Corps (RAMC).

The basic medical unit was the Regimental Aid Post (RAP), which accompanied an infantry battalion into the fighting. It consisted of the Regimental Medical Officer (RMO) assisted by two orderlies, one of whom was trained to look after surgical and medical equipment and assist the doctor. There were also usually 16 (combatant) stretcher-bearers per infantry battalion. They were not members of the AAMC, but were either infantrymen or bandsmen trained in first aid who would put aside their arms and don a Red Cross brassard in time of battle.

---

1   MacPherson, W. and Mitchell, T.J. (eds.), *History of the Great War – Medical Services,* Twelve volumes, HMSO, London, 1931, p.198.

Sir William Williams, KCMG, 1856-1919 AAMC

Born in Sydney on 20 July 1856, Williams was educated at Sydney Grammar School before graduating from London University College Medical School at 24 years of age. He was appointed Principal Medical Officer for a small contingent of troops New South Wales deployed to the Sudan in 1885. In 1893 Williams suggested a motto for the New South Wales Army Medical Corps, which was subsequently adopted by the Australian Army Medical Corps (now the RAAMC). He proposed '*Paulatim*', a Latin word that reflected the short history and subsequent growth of the corps up to that time – 'little by little'. Williams deployed again to the second Boer War, where he distinguished himself by his focus on highly mobile field medical units and casualty evacuation. By 1914 he was arguably too old for field command and was soon superseded by the dynamic Neville Howse, the first Australian to be awarded a Victoria Cross.

Above: Sir William Williams, KCMG, 1856-1919 AAMC. (RAAMC Museum Bandiana)

The RMO was responsible for selecting a site for his RAP or dressing station, which could be a tent, dugout or sheltered gully. It was there that stretcher-bearers brought their wounded. At the RAP casualties were given such first aid as was possible and triaged (or sorted) according to the severity of their wound or condition. Soldiers with minor wounds were treated, and wherever possible returned to duty. Members of a larger unit called a field ambulance (Fd Amb) evacuated badly wounded or seriously ill casualties to the rear.

A field ambulance generally consisted of ten officers and 224 ORs organised in two parts: a 'tent subdivision' (nursing and administration), and a 'bearer subdivision' consisting of three sections (A, B and C), each of which was equipped to hold and care for 50 casualties, but only for periods of up to three days.

Wounded men were moved as infrequently as possible. To this end, a casualty was kept on the same stretcher from the time he left the RAP until he was carried to the field ambulance – or at least that was the doctrinal view. Bearers were then supposed to be given a stretcher in return from the stock held by the ambulance. As we shall see, such was the chaos and demand at Gallipoli that this system quickly broke down, resulting in shortages of stretchers when they were most needed.

The next unit in the organisational hierarchy was the casualty clearing station (CCS), which was capable of providing 200 beds. It was staffed by eight officers and 77 ORs. As the name suggests, its purpose was to clear the ambulances of their casualties, thus ensuring unimpeded traffic of bearers to and from the front lines. It was responsible for the care of wounded of all categories until evacuation was completed behind the lines, or along the Lines of Communication.

Lines of Communication is an important military concept. It refers to the system of communication by foot, road or sea between an army (in this case on Gallipoli), its advance base (Imbros), intermediate base (the island of Lemnos, 111 kilometres from Gallipoli), and the major logistic bases at Alexandria and Cairo in Egypt, or the Royal Navy (RN) base at Malta. Map 1.1 shows the overall area of operations, while Map 1.2 provides an idea of distances involved. Then, as now, distance and time were of prime concern to the medical services, and often dictated survival rates for badly wounded or seriously ill soldiers.

A stationary hospital was the next largest unit, and it approximated to what we would recognise as a fair sized civilian hospital. Nos. 1, 2, and 3 Australian Stationary Hospitals (ASHs) were deployed on Lemnos at various times, and were for the most part under canvas. Theoretically they were placed at or in front of the advanced base (Alexandria) to receive casualties with minor injuries and illnesses, who could be treated, nursed, and returned to the front in a relatively short time.

The largest unit of the AAMC was the Australian General Hospital (AGH). These units were the equivalent of major city hospitals, with medical and surgical departments, laboratories, etc. They were usually organised on the basis of 520 beds. No. 1 AGH in Cairo, however, grew to accommodate some 3,500 beds within months of its arrival there. Other AGHs later set up nearby experienced similar growth, as the numbers of casualties grew during 1915.

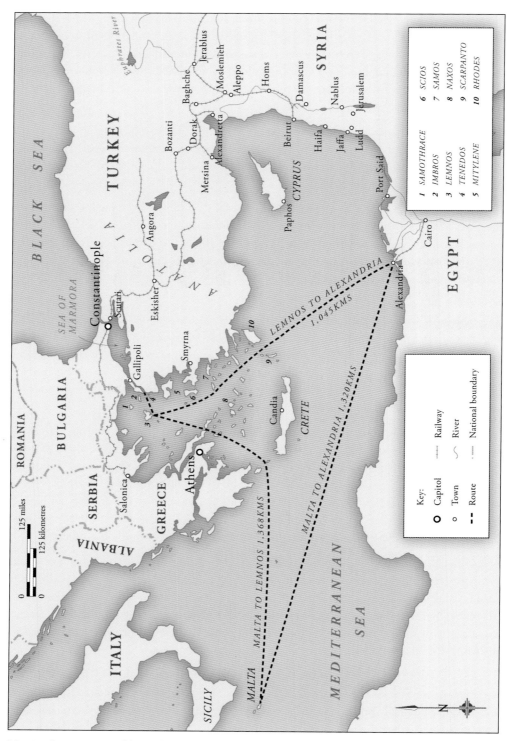

Map 1.1. Operations area of the Mediterranean Expeditionary Force.

A group of Australian Army nurses and members of the AAMC aboard the troopship *Omrah en route* to Egypt late 1914. (AWM C02538)

The medical service of the Ottoman army was well organised centrally, but it had to face insoluble problems. Also, it could not conduct any preventative health work, because the British naval blockade prevented it obtaining medical supplies and instruments until later in the war, when Germany and Austria could supply drugs and materiel overland.

Each infantry division in the Ottoman army was authorised a field medical unit, and each corps four field hospitals. However these were never staffed to established strengths. This deficiency was compounded by chronic shortages of medicine and medical supplies caused by the British naval blockade in the Mediterranean. The total Ottoman military hospital capacity was 37,000 beds, of which 14,000 were located in Constantinople (now Istanbul) to the north of the Gallipoli peninsula.

The Ottoman army had no motorised transport. The lack of wagons and draft animals for medical transportation (indeed for transportation for all purposes) was a critical weakness. Since the medical companies of the Ottoman units on Gallipoli usually had no transportation at their disposal, their sick and wounded had to be carried to the medical units located behind the lines by transportation convoys normally carrying ammunition.

The Ottoman military medical service also suffered from a shortage of doctors. The number of physicians for the entire army totalled 2555, including 1202 professional army 'surgeons' and 1353 reservist doctors.

Matron Grace Wilson, CBE, 1879-1957

Born in Brisbane, Wilson studied nursing both there and in London. At the outbreak of war she was matron of the Brisbane Hospital. She joined the newly formed Australian Army Nursing Service in 1914. An extremely able woman and leader, she was matron of No. 3 Australian General Hospital under canvas on Lemnos. She saw active service in the Middle East during World War II.

Above: Matron Grace Wilson, CBE, 1879-1957. (AWM A05332)

Ottoman Red Crescent members on the Gallipoli front.

BACKGROUND AND MOTIVES OF MEDICAL CORPS RECRUITS

Members of the AAMC who served on or near Gallipoli were from a variety of backgrounds. Like the rest of the AIF, they reflected the society from which they came. Many were recent migrants from Britain; almost all were white.

In March 1915 the 2nd Light Horse (LH) Fd Amb's nominal roll showed that of 126 men, only 14 were married, and most enlisted in October/November 1914. Despite belonging to a horsed brigade there were many town dwellers among them, including students and clerks, but very few stockmen or bushmen. A great many were much older than fresh faced 18 year olds.

The motives of these volunteers were probably those of Australian Diggers generally in 1914: the desire to be in the same unit as one's mates, to use their civilian skills (first aid), or enact humanitarian ideals. Others were attracted to the regular pay; some were simply bored with their humdrum lives; others wanted to evade the police or creditors.

One man joined a field ambulance because his local doctor had joined that unit. Another noted in his diary that he enlisted in the AIF, 'but owing to my father's prejudice against my joining a fighting unit had to go into the AMC'. For many it 'was just being faced with the ordinary never changing things of life … I wanted the thrill of something new …' For others it was a happier alternative to unemployment.

Not everyone found enlisting an easy matter. One recruit arrived at Victoria Barracks in Sydney before having second thoughts. He eventually enlisted after a great deal of hesitation. Others were keener: 'It was not long before I made up my mind to be "Up and at 'em", for I am British born …'

Nearer the Dardanelles other men found that they had made the wrong choice. The officer commanding No. 1 ASH at Mudros wrote of one of his privates who had 'been twice punished for drunkenness and once for breaking bounds and drunkenness since February 1st 1915. He is useless for hospital work and himself desires transference into a combat unit'.

The pressures to enlist extended to students at universities and medical schools, and a number left their studies to join the ranks. The authorities, alarmed at the potential loss of future doctors, tried to counter the drain. Towards the end of 1915 the army commenced returning from hospitals in Egypt all former medical students who were sick, wounded or convalescent, so that they might finish their course.

The Council of the University of Melbourne also amended its Medical Faculty Regulations at a meeting on 7 July 1915, reducing the length of its course from five years to four years and one term. The medical faculty lost four of its graduates, three first-year medical students, two second-year students, and one from the fifth year at Gallipoli.

On the home front social pressure, including the attitudes of women, were not unimportant considerations. At the height of the Gallipoli campaign Matron Grace Wilson of No.3 AGH on Lemnos wrote home: 'My opinion of any man who stays, unless absolutely prevented from going isn't much – that is to say unmarried men – the others can do their duty otherwise – and can keep things going in their own countries'. Conformity and duty to king and country were also popular clerical themes. The Melbourne *Age* newspaper reported a sermon in which the clergyman declared that the: 'man who is not fighting is already slackening and decadent'.

Medics and stretcher-bearers received only the basics of first aid training. To the modern eye the training schedules seem very simple indeed. In 1914-15, teaching the syllabus for a medical unit's training took a mere two weeks. The first half of each day's training was devoted to stretcher, squad and company drills and signalling.

In the afternoon practical instruction was given in first aid based on the 1911 *RAMC Training Manual*. This manual was standard throughout the Empire. Additional lectures were given by specialists in different fields, for example anatomy and physiology, military law, the care of the horse, and clerical duties. In some circumstances men recruited directly into a medical unit, and who were considered suitable, might then receive further training in a civilian hospital.

At the regimental level the suggested training was also based on the RAMC manual. There were practical sessions on packing and unloading equipment, signalling (semaphore), collecting wounded, and various ways of transporting them by foot. Other recruits went through a different process. For example, when No.1 ASH started selecting its personnel on 10 September 1914, the first men taken on were recruits who had originally applied to join the 4th Fd Amb, but who were turned away when it had filled its establishment.

Many contemporary accounts illustrate the real lack of preparation for wartime duties in medical units. Typical of this situation was the 4th Fd Amb, which was mobilised at Broadmeadows, near Melbourne, late in 1914. The unit's transport section had the added difficulty of having to break in their horses, which were drawn unbroken from remount depots.

Sir Neville Howse, VC, KCMG, KCB, KStJ, 1863-1930

Born in England in 1863, Howse qualified as a surgeon in London before migrating to Australia. He saw service in the second Boer War, and was awarded a Victoria Cross for retrieving a casualty under heavy fire. He accompanied the Australian Naval and Military Expeditionary Force to New Guinea in 1914, but was soon bored through lack of activity. Well connected and extremely able, it was not long before he superseded Williams as Director of Medical Services for the AIF. He spent several months on Gallipoli as the senior medical officer of the 1st Australian Division.

The men recruited as ORs into medical units often had basic first aid knowledge. This had been provided by the St. John Ambulance Association, as the Red Cross was not widely established outside New South Wales before August 1914. St. John Ambulance had trained workers in State railway systems and men and women in most towns.

On the outbreak of war St. John Ambulance furnished a valuable reservoir of skilled recruits for the medical services, and the training given by it proved invaluable in the field. Early in the war the Adelaide branch advertised for a number of certificated men and women to volunteer to travel to the Mediterranean theatre as auxiliaries with the AAMC. This offer was, however, declined by the army.

The method of selecting a man for regimental medical duties varied from unit to unit. Often it was simply a matter of an officer or NCO nominating a number of men. Others chose more carefully, as Major L.O. Betts, a light horse medical officer wrote: 'Four from each Squadron, or twelve in all were chosen by troop leaders very often because they were not much use in the troop. Later we increased the number to eight per squadron and as at that time I had more experience, I insisted that men with more than average intelligence be detached from the work'. They were trained by Betts using lectures, demonstrations and drills based on the RAMC manual.

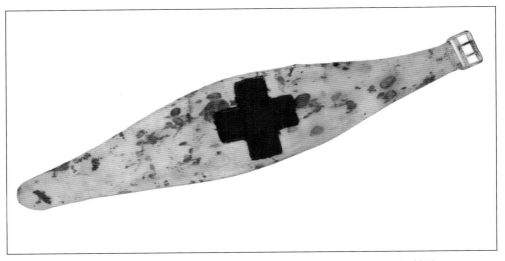

A Red Cross brassard worn by Private Harold May, 3rd Australian Field Ambulance. (AWM REL34450)

In 1914 and 1915 Australian nurses were recruited both from the tiny Army Nursing Service and from civilian nursing groups. Military medical training was somewhat light in terms of both content and frequency. Before 1915 the Army Nursing Service had undertaken 'practically no peace training and had no pay, not even for expenses'. This was remarked on, and was in stark contrast to the (British) Queen Alexandra's Imperial Military Nursing Service, which had a permanent cadre staff, and whose members were thoroughly trained in military procedure and administration. They had less trouble working with both medical and combatant male officers.

Female nurses played an extremely important part in World War I. However, only a relatively small number of Australian nurses were employed near the front during the Gallipoli campaign (on Lemnos). Many worked further back in the Lines of Communication, and did invaluable work in hospitals at Alexandria and Cairo.

That so few were deployed closer to the front in 1915 may be partly explained by the attitudes of senior medical officers (both Australian and British), as well as their largely untried capacity in the period preceding the massive campaigns on the Western Front from 1916. These views were widely held, and were typical of contemporary social mores within male army circles. While officially the services of female doctors were refused, there were too few in Australia at that time for this to become an issue, as it did in Britain.

Training was very basic for all ranks in the AAMC. For their part, doctors received little in the way of military skills. Most doctors, orderlies and nurses had until very recently been civilians, with no military training. Medical officers themselves later realised that inadequate training may have explained some of the errors that occurred on Gallipoli.

Colonel Neville Howse, VC, of the AAMC who, as Assistant Director of Medical Services (ADMS) of the 1st Division was the senior Australian medical officer on Gallipoli, received a letter from one of his officers in which the latter bemoaned the lack of adequate training in military medicine at home. This man, an RMO, had learned nothing of public health, and although most AIF medical reinforcements had been serving in Australia or in ships and hospitals after their enlistment, none had been trained in preventative health measures. Prevention was at the core of any medical organisation's responsibilities, and played a central role on Gallipoli.

Members of the 2nd Australian Field Ambulance manning the oars in Lemnos harbour. (AWM C01632)

GALLIPOLI AS AN ALLIED STRATEGY

There is little point trying to duplicate here the hundreds of books written about why Britain (with French assistance) decided to begin an offensive against Turkey using the Gallipoli peninsula as a launching point. Suffice it to say that responsibility (or lack of it) for the concept of operations has been laid at the feet of several individuals or institutions. These include the First Lord of the Admiralty, Winston Churchill, the First Sea Lord, Admiral 'Jackie' Fisher, David Lloyd George, Field Marshal Lord Kitchener, Prime Minister Herbert Asquith, and a weak and vacillating British War Council.

Common to all, perhaps, was a desire to break the deadlock of the Western Front. By delivering a decisive blow against Turkey, the allies might gain a strategic advantage while also opening imperial Russia to imports of much needed wheat and munitions through the Black Sea. There were also the spoils to be had in dismembering the crumbling Ottoman Empire - the 'sick man of Europe'. In 1914 an attack on Gallipoli was very much an on-again off-again affair, and was always going to be a purely naval operation.

A paper drawn up by the general staff in 1906 had concluded that a successful attack directed against the Gallipoli peninsula depended upon the fleet silencing any opposition completely before and during the landing of troops. In view of the risks involved the general staff at that time was 'not prepared to recommend its being attempted'. In 1914, however, support for the campaign gained an impetus of its own, and by February 1915 it had become a reality in which the army, rather than the navy, had the central role.

First aid and stretcher carry drills being practised by members of the 1st Battalion in Egypt, early 1915. (AWM P07973.010)

The command of the Mediterranean Expeditionary Force (MEF) was given to General Sir Ian Hamilton. As he knew that all hopes of a surprise landing had long ago evaporated, his plan was to land his Anglo-French forces at six different locations in order to confuse the enemy as to his main effort. In this he was to be supported by the fire power of the navy.

The allied plan involved three parts, the centrepiece of which was a landing at Z or Brighton Beach by Major-General William Bridges' 1st Division to capture the ridge called Sari Bair. The New Zealand and Australian (NZ&A) Division under Major-General Sir Alexander Godley would then continue the advance to seize the Mal Tepe plateau (which overlooked the narrows on the east of the Gallipoli peninsula), cutting the peninsula in two. The arc of Sir William Birdwood's proposed front extended from the fortified cape of Gabe Tepe in the south to Hill 971 (Koja Cimen Tepe) a little over three kilometres north - a line about two kilometres in from the landing beach.

In the second part of the plan the 29th British Division would land at Cape Helles on the peninsula's southern-most tip, while across the Narrows on the Asiatic shore the newly formed French *Corps Expéditionnaire d'Orient* under General Albert d'Amade landed at Kum Kale to draw enemy reserves to reinforce the forts there. After several days the French force would withdraw and rejoin the British. The plan worked to the extent that it did confuse the enemy, but it only succeeded in delaying any timely counter-attack in force.

Opposing the allies were the men of the newly formed Ottoman *Fifth Army*, which consisted chiefly of the highly trained *III Corps* under Major-General Esat Pasha defending the peninsula, and *XV Corps* on the Asiatic coast. The *5th Division* and a cavalry brigade formed the army's reserve.

Major-General Esat Pasha.

Esat deployed his *7th Division* on the isthmus at Bulair, and the *9th Division* to the southern tip of the peninsula. He held the *19th Division* (almost 11,000 men) in the centre as a corps reserve, and it was this formation that stopped Birdwood's attacking force in its tracks. It is important to note that the Ottoman forces remained outnumbered through most of the Gallipoli campaign.

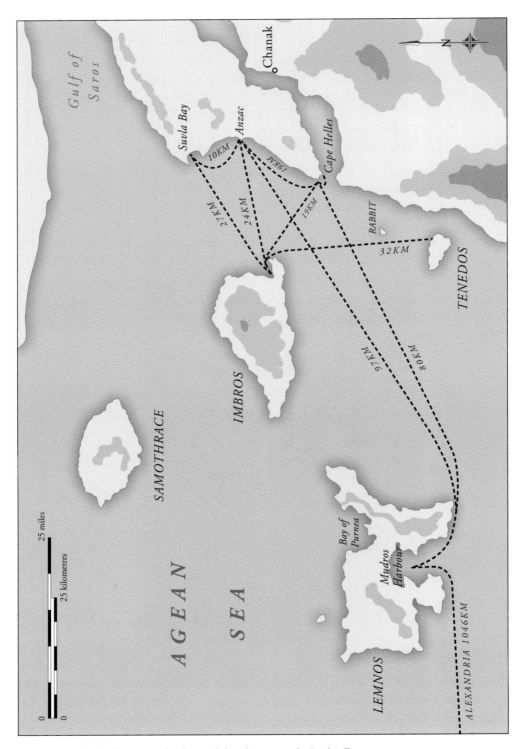

Map 1.2. The islands of Lemnos and Imbros and their distances to the Dradanelles.

General Sir Ian Hamilton, GCB, GCMG, DSO 1853-1947

Hamilton had served in the Afghan War and the first and second Boer Wars. He visited Australia in 1914 in his role as Inspector General of Overseas Forces. Highly educated, he was probably out of his depth for the type of command required at Gallipoli. Hamilton kept himself aloof from most events on the peninsula, preferring to stay with his headquarters on HMS *Queen Elizabeth*.

Source: http://en.wikipedia.org/wiki/Ian_Standish_Monteith_Hamilton

HASTE AND IGNORANCE

Three factors determined the medical response over the following nine months. The first was Hamilton's decision in March to set sail for the theatre of operations while leaving his administrative staff in Alexandria. The second was Hamilton's personal remoteness and inaccessibility – an isolation jealously guarded by his inner circle.

The general staff went first to Alexandria, then to Lemnos, to organise the Gallipoli landings. Neither the Quartermaster-General (QMG), the Adjutant-General (AG), nor the Director of Medical Services (DMS), however, was represented at a senior level until the eve of the landing. When they arrived in the theatre, they found that the general staff had already begun making administrative arrangements, most of which were fundamentally flawed. To be fair, the medical planners had no experience on which to draw. The most recent 'comparable' event was the French landing at Algiers in 1830.

The third factor was the lack of communications, about which more will be said later.

LINES OF COMMUNICATION MEDICAL ORGANISATION

Behind the scenes were the AIF bases at Alexandria and Cairo in Egypt, where a senior British medical officer, Surgeon-General Sir R.W. Ford, was chief medical officer for the British commander there, General Sir John Maxwell.

At the beginning of 1915, the AAMC was to be absorbed entirely into the MEF, morphing into an Imperial organisation. Australian authorities were responsible for raising, equipping and training Australian medical units, but once those units arrived in Egypt, they immediately came under Ford's control.

Unfortunately, senior British officers in Egypt assumed that the AIF would continue to be responsible for the internal administration of the AAMC units under British control. In Egypt, especially, a great deal of animosity and criticism was caused when Australian medical units came under the direct supervision of British medical officers. One Australian doctor noted that 'It is hard being under RAMC men who though quite nice know not the officers nor the organisation and constitution and don't try very hard to find out'.

In a letter to Colonel Richard Fetherston, the senior medical officer in Australia, Colonel Cyril Brudenell White (chief of staff to Bridges) wrote that the:

> cost to Australia of medical arrangements in Egypt is enormous. All that cost is at present being incurred by RAMC officers who are not responsible for their action to the Australian Government ... From the Australian point of view this alone makes provision of some effective administrative machinery, a necessity.

Unfortunately that machinery, in the form of the AAMC's own senior commander (a situation enjoyed by the Canadians), did not materialise until Howse was appointed DMS, AIF in November 1915. Until then, there was no senior Australian medical officer in Egypt responsible for the Australian forces there.

Australian military authorities contributed to the confusion by not supporting their own DGMS, Williams, when he arrived in Egypt early in 1915. Fetherston was convinced that it would have been much better if the Defence Department in Melbourne had initially insisted that in Australian matters the AAMC would do things in its own way. The Australian Government dithered, however, and could not decide.

Ford, the DMS (Cairo), controlled all medical arrangements there. He was the senior medical officer in Egypt, on the staff of GHQ Egypt, but was unaware of the confusion in Australia. For the operations of the MEF, however, the senior army medical officer was Surgeon-General William Birrell, the DMS, MEF, who had been brought out of retirement.

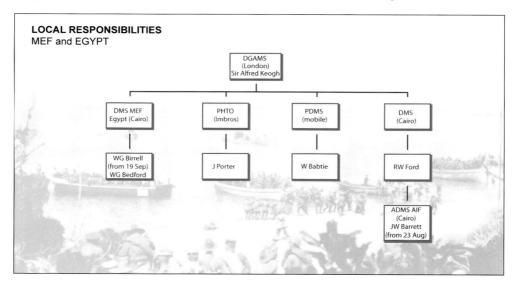

In June, in a belated attempt to address rising public disquiet in Britain and the Dominions at what was only then being revealed publicly of the April landings, the British Principal Director of Medical Services (PDMS), Surgeon-General William Babtie, who arrived in June, was appointed to coordinate all medical arrangements in the Mediterranean. A little later the navy followed suit, appointing Surgeon Vice-Admiral Sir James Porter as its Principal Hospital Transport Officer (PHTO).

Babtie was the first officer to hold the appointment of PDMS for the Levant. The establishment of this post was the result of an attempt by the War Office to resolve the medical problems that occurred in April. The navy, unaware of Babtie and his role, appointed Porter for much the same reason, but his arrival in Egypt on 24 July only added to the confusion. Their areas of responsibility were not clear, particularly where inter-Service cooperation and liaison at senior command level were required.

Despite overlapping responsibilities, the appointment of these officers resulted in some improvements. Babtie arranged for more hospital ships and medical staff, and expanded hospital accommodation on Lemnos. Porter, for his part, was responsible for more efficient medical evacuation by sea.

Lieutenant General Sir William Babtie, VC, KCB, KCMG, 1859-1920

Like Howse, Babtie was awarded his VC during the second Boer War. Before the Gallipoli Campaign he was briefly in charge of the Indian Army Medical Services. Babtie was out of his depth in an operation as complex as Gallipoli, and was officially and publicly criticised for his role in casualty evacuation.

General Sir William Babtie. (Wellcome Library, London, V0025984)

To summarise, a naval surgeon was appointed over an army doctor to take charge of a medical evacuation scheme designed along vague lines by the army, using the resources of the navy. Neither medical arm of the two services had worked with the other on such a scale before. Added to this was the failure by the War Office to notify all senior officers of Porter's appointment, an omission that heightened personal animosities among senior staff officers.

TABLE 2.0: IMPORTANT EVENTS AND DATES FOR THE MEDICAL SERVICES

	1914
Britain declares war on the German and Austrian Empires	4 AUG
Turkey enters the war	31 OCT
The first AIF leaves Australia by convoy	1 NOV
Last units of the 1st AIF disembarked at Alexandria, Egypt	4 DEC
	1915
The No.1 Australian General Hospital arrives in Egypt	13 JAN
Surgeon- General W. Birrell takes control of the Medical arrangements of the MEF	1 APR
First Landings at Gallipoli	25 APR
Second Battle of Krithia	6-8 MAY
Colonel Neville Manders NZAMC is killed	7 AUG
German Submarines sighted	12 MAY
The Mooltan arrives from Australia with Medical reinforcements	16 JUN
Surgeon-General Babtie, Principal Director Medical Services arrives in Egypt	24 JUN
Vice Admiral Porter, Principal Hostpital Transport Officer, arrives in Egypt	24 JUL
Battles of Lone Pine, Sari Bair and Suvla Bay	6-8 AUG
Colonel Howse replaces Gereral Williams AS DMS, AIF	1 DEC
Commencement of the first phase of the Evacuation of Gallipoli	6-13 DEC
The last men withdraw from the Peninsula	20 DEC

Let us go back a little. On 24 February 1915, Surgeon-General Sir Alfred Keogh, Director-General of the British Army Medical Service (DGAMS) at the War Office, nominated Colonel J. Maher (later superseded by Birrell) as DMS for the MEF.

On 15 March Maher arrived at Mudros, on Lemnos to report on its suitability as a base from a medical and health perspective. He advised that it was unsuitable because of the lack of potable water. Consequently, Mudros and its huge but undeveloped harbour were intended to be used solely as a base for assembling troops immediately before the landing. At this time no provision was made for the long-term establishment of any medical unit of significant size on Lemnos. When more experienced officers arrived in theatre this changed, however, and No. 1 ASH was deployed there in mid-March.

Both Birrell and Babtie, who was responsible for casualty movement, answered directly to the War Office. For his part Birdwood did nothing to support Williams or plead for Australian autonomy in this matter. In retrospect, this was a failure of command. The result was that Ford rapidly took all the Australian military hospitals and their staff under his direct control. The problem was compounded by the absence of a Deputy Director of Medical Services (DDMS) ANZAC or an ADMS 1st Division appointment early in the campaign.

15 April, a view of part of Mudros harbour with troops about to embark. (AWM PO2934.019)

This was not the fault of senior British medical officers, either on Gallipoli or in Britain. Rather it lay in the first instance with both Colonel Neville Manders (the senior medical officer of the ANZAC) and Howse (his counterpart in the 1st Division) for refusing the DDMS appointment in April, and later with Hamilton, who prevented any officer being appointed as DDMS ANZAC.

FINAL PREPARATIONS

Hamilton, who had spent some time in Australia in 1914, stayed several days at Mudros, using it as a base from which to conduct his first reconnaissance of the Gallipoli peninsula by ship on 18 March. On 22 March he returned to Egypt to finalise arrangements for the invasion. During this period Hamilton had almost no planning assistance, as his key administrative staff were still *en route* from Britain.

Partly on the basis of Maher's appreciation of Lemnos, Hamilton redeployed his advanced base rearward from Lemnos to Alexandria, 1200 kilometres from Gallipoli. The Royal Naval Division and the French Corps, which had earlier been deployed to Mudros, were also sent back to Egypt.

Australia's 3rd Brigade, however, remained on transport ships in Mudros Bay, landing battalions for exercises on shore as the weather and sea conditions permitted. This haphazard, and often disorganised, approach to planning continued through most of 1915. The Ottoman command structure, particularly at army level, operated at much higher levels of effectiveness than its British counterpart, and generally had greater situational and spatial awareness.

The enemy forces were also well prepared. The German commander of the *Fifth Army*, General Otto Liman Von Sanders, arrived in the town of Gallipoli on the eastern shore of the Gallipoli peninsula on March 26, and set up his headquarters there. After numerous naval attacks by the allies over the preceding months, it was no surprise that the peninsula would be the most likely site for an enemy landing.

Liman Von Sanders concentrated on preparations that were within Ottoman capabilities, such as improving the local road network, camouflaging troop concentrations and artillery batteries, and improving fortifications along the likely landing beaches. Medical preparations were made too, so that by mid-March 1915 there was a total of 1050 beds available to treat casualties.

Not everyone was comfortable with the medical aspects of the campaign, then or later. The British official medical history concluded that the medical side of the campaign did not seem to have been thoroughly thought out. It stated that, although the treatment of the wounded on the Gallipoli peninsula might have been as satisfactory as circumstances would permit, many of the complaints about the transport of casualties to the ships, and then to Egypt, Malta and Britain, were justified.

The allies' medical preparations were effectively hamstrung, because neither the British nor the Australian and New Zealand medical services were privy to the landing plan. Hamilton's intentions, his objectives, and the strategies with which these were to be implemented, were never clearly articulated before the Gallipoli operations.

When Hamilton left for Lemnos in April, he did not even indicate where he expected allied casualties to be sent: Egypt, Malta, or Britain. Nor, at that time, did he request that hospital accommodation be prepared for any specific number of casualties until his staff came up with a plan initially based on a casualty estimate of 3000 casualties, or 5.5 percent of his force of about 75,000 troops (35,000 British, 32,000 Australians and 7500 New Zealanders). The French corps had its own arrangements.

Even before the landing, life was far from comfortable for those Diggers already in hospital on Lemnos. An entry in the war diary of No. 1 ASH for 9 April 1915 reads: 'Hurricane & rain during night 6 tents blown down. Men up all night shifting patients'. Then on 21 April this hospital 'Informed DMS cannot accommodate any more patients'. Only a week earlier 183 patients were cleared to Alexandria on the troop ship *Osmanieh*. However, by this time there were no hospital ships to take the overflow.

It would be a daunting prospect, even today, to coordinate the medical services for such a large-scale amphibious operation. Those in charge expected it would be a 'short, sharp action', which would take more than enough ground to ensure the landing of the force and its equipment and, importantly, everything the medical services would need, including wheeled transport and the ability to deploy larger units such as stationary hospitals. Unfortunately, all the ground gained for this purpose at Anzac Cove turned out to be a narrow pebbly beach, in some places only a few metres wide.

The 3rd Brigade, which was to spearhead Birdwood's attack on Gaba Tepe, had been at Mudros since the first week of March practising day and night operations. No. 1 ASH had followed with 200 tonnes of equipment, arriving on 15 March. Five days later it was accommodating 120 sick. Mudros harbour soon began to fill with assorted ships, until by the middle of April it contained over 108 troop and transport ships, warships, and other vessels. The 29th British Division was packed onto 20 troopships and the ANZAC on 40 others. All retained their own sick aboard.

The landing was originally scheduled for 21 April, but was postponed due to appalling weather. This date explains the alarmed protestations made both by senior medical staff and the Deputy Adjutant-General (DAG), Brigadier-General E.M. Woodward, who was ultimately responsible for the evacuation of wounded.

Bad weather also hampered attempts at coordinated training exercises (boat drill, route marches and stretcher drill ashore, and practising embarking wounded up gangways, by derricks and slings), which could not be carried out with much thoroughness. The situation immediately before the landing was further compromised by the lack of available time (approximately a week) to reorganise units scattered across numerous ships while relying almost entirely on flag or semaphore signals to communicate.

On Friday 23 April the storm cleared and the senior naval commander at the Dardanelles, Vice-Admiral Sir John De Robeck, issued orders that the landing would take place on the 25th. As the armada left the harbour, a conference was held aboard the *Lutzow* at which all the senior Australian and New Zealand officers, including those of the medical services, were present. Only then were the details of the landing, together with military objectives, outlined for the first time. Even so, there was almost no opportunity for the commanders of the field ambulances to consult with their brigades' medical officers and RMOs, so the latter remained largely ignorant of the wider medical and operational plan.

CHAPTER 2:

The Landing and Consolidation

For much of the Gallipoli campaign the AAMC had to deal with shortcomings in higher command and strategy, and in the administration of supplies, both areas critical to the medical effort, but beyond the control of Australian medical officers and units on the peninsula. The first major problems arose during and after the landing on 25 April 1915.

THE LANDING

Before dawn on Sunday 25 April, men of the 3rd Brigade splashed ashore. The place was a narrow beach at Ari Burnu, on the west coast of the Gallipoli peninsula, known to us as Anzac Cove. For medical support it had the brigade's RMO Captain W. Mainwaring and his small team, the 3rd Fd Amb (commanded by Lieutenant-Colonel Alfred Sutton), which lost three men killed and 14 wounded, and the brigade's stretcher-bearers. For a number of reasons (which are still disputed), the force was landed two kilometres further north than intended.

This was just as well, for had they arrived at the intended landing point at Brighton Beach, further south, the attackers would have been met by *5 Company* of Lieutenant-Colonel Mehmet Şefik's *2/27 Regiment* (*9th Division*), under an experienced commander, occupying well prepared and sited positions dating from 1912. Ottoman units along the western coast of the peninsula had spent months improving both their positions and their communications.

Defending Ottoman units opened fire on the attackers at 0420 and, as daylight broke, this was supplemented by effective shrapnel fire from supporting artillery further south. Tactically, the *Fifth Army* on Gallipoli had deployed a light infantry screen in outposts sited on the dominating terrain overlooking potential landing beaches. These forces were usually in platoon strength, and were in prepared trenches, with wire laid.

The Ottoman forces did not intend these troops to stop the allies on the beaches. Regiment-sized forces were positioned three to five kilometres behind the beaches on protected higher ground. As the outposts slowed the enemy landing and channelled their advance, these larger forces would then counter-attack.

When the British forces appeared at the entrance of the Dardanelles Strait the Ottoman army had deployed five infirmaries, each of 150 beds, along the peninsula and the Asiatic shore, and one 250-bed *Mevkii* (local) hospital. Local diseases included malaria, cholera, typhoid and smallpox. Typhus, tuberculosis (TB), pneumonia and pleurisy were also common in the region, and lice were endemic.

Medium Machine-gun, Maschinengewehr 08/15

The *Maschinengewehr* 08 (MG08) Maxim machine-gun was almost a copy of Hiram S. Maxim's original 1884 Maxim gun. It was a bulky, heavy, short recoil operated, water-cooled, fully automatic belt-fed machine-gun. Using a separate attachment sight with range calculator for indirect fire, the MG08 was often operated from cover behind the forward German trench-line. The MG08 was usually issued on a sled-type mount of adjustable height (*SchlittenLafette* 08). This mount allowed the gun to be dragged through the battlefield or carried like a stretcher by two or more soldiers. The mount was provided with traverse and elevation mechanisms with rough and fine adjustments. Alternatively, the MG08 could be installed on a tripod mount commercially developed by DWM. One of Germany's most important weapons in the First World War, it was ubiquitous on the Western Front in 1916, with 3,000 units produced each month in that year. By the Battle of Fromelles, the German Army had established a deadly network of machinegun posts in front of the British line, using a combination of enfilade, indirect and direct fire, and intersecting arcs with riflemen support.

Calibre: 7.92mm Mauser
Weight: 26.5kg gun body, 4kg water, 38.5kg tripod
Rate of fire: Cyclic – 450rpm
Effective Range: 2000m (max on tripod mount 3600m)
Manufacturer: Deutsche Waffen und Munitionsfabriken (DWM) and Spandau Arsenal, Germany

Length: 1.175m
Action: Recoil
Feed system: 250 round cloth belt

The deadly Maxim *Maschinengewehr* '08. While the Ottoman army was in short supply of these weapons, they caused serious death and injuries to thousands of troops. (Mark Wahlert)

Once elements of the 3rd Fd Amb landed, they took shelter under the cliffs at the back of the beach. Virtually trapped, they could do little more than attend to their own wounded, as their position was subjected to heavy sniping. When this eased they set to work improving shelter, establishing collecting posts, and attending to and bringing in nearby wounded. Officers and sergeants then went out with small squads of medics to search as far as possible along the shore and over the hills, looking for wounded.

When the Diggers leapt off their boats in the half-light, they were confronted with sheer cliffs; almost impenetrable prickly scrub; and a murderous hail of machine-gun fire and shrapnel from the Ottoman positions above. A number were killed in their boats; others were struck down while wading ashore. Cries of 'Stretcher-bearer!' went up, but were unheeded for a time, as medics and regimental stretcher-bearers were also hit as they landed. Artillery caused many casualties, and it was fortunate for the invaders that the Ottoman guns had to carefully husband their ammunition because of the limited quantities on hand.

The 2nd Brigade landed between 0500 and 0730, followed by the 2nd Fd Amb (under Lieutenant-Colonel A. Sturdee) at 0630. Between 0900 and 1200 the Auckland Battalion and three battalions of the 1st Brigade, with its 1st Fd Amb (Lieutenant-Colonel Brian Newmarch), landed. The bearer subdivisions, without their equipment, landed with their brigades.

All three medical units concentrated their efforts on two gullies soon tagged as Shrapnel Valley and Monash Valley. Howse landed at 0730 with Divisional Headquarters (HQ). He immediately reconnoitred a suitable area and placed No.1 Australian CCS (ACCS), commanded by Lieutenant-Colonel William Giblin, on a part of the beach protected by MacLagan's Ridge.

The topography and terrain of Anzac Cove largely determined the collecting of wounded and the course of medical evacuation. By noon all RMOs had set up their RAPs, and were attending to more serious cases in dressing stations while they waited for stretcher-bearers from their field ambulances to come forward to collect casualties. Walking wounded were directed to the beach for attention. All medical arrangements for the landing were based on the sensible premise that until the tactical situation became clearer, only an absolute minimum of medical personnel and equipment could be taken ashore on the first day.

THE FIRST FORTY-EIGHT HOURS

This diary entry for the 1st Fd Amb is typical of those medical units which landed on 25 April: '0930. Much heavy fire. Commenced work and continued between the firing line and the beach until midnight after which the men were divided into details and thus ensured continuance of work and a slight amount of rest …'

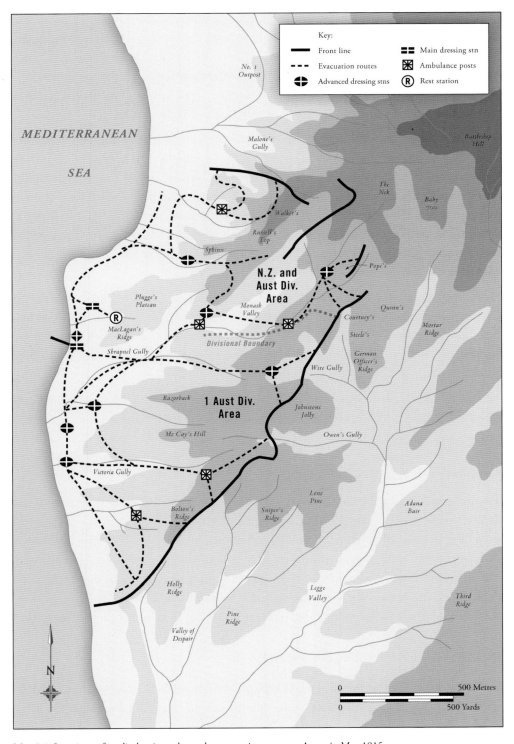

Map 2.1. Locations of medical units and casualty evacuation routes at Anzac in May 1915.

The Krupp 120mm Model 1905

The Krupp 120mm Model 1905 was a howitzer manufactured by the famous German armaments company Krupp. This model was an "off the shelf" model which could be quickly dispatched to client armies.

It differed from much of the artillery of this size used on the Western Front in that it had no gun shield for its crew.

Weight: 1,125 kg,
Muzzle velocity: 275 m/s (900 ft/s)
Range: 5,800 m (6,300 yds).

A German manufactured Krupp 77mm field gun as used by the Ottoman forces at Gallipoli. Many casualties were sustained in the first few days from Ottoman artillery fire. Shrapnel wounds caused havoc for surgeons in the primitive conditions. (Mark Wahlert)

Part of the 4th Battalion and mules of the 26th Indian Mountain Battery landing at Anzac Cove at 0800 on 25 April. In the foreground are staff of the 1st Brigade. (IWM Q112876)

RAPs were established in any sheltered spot, and stretcher-bearers attached themselves to small bodies of troops who desperately sought to gain a toehold on the slopes. Wounded Diggers were attended to, and the locations of the RAPs were sent back to the ADMS on the beach, so he could track the location and movement of all medical units. He could also arrange for medical and other equipment to be sent where needed. The problem was that, because of the poor quality maps and the difficult ground, few RAPs, let alone combatant units, knew where they were. The result was chaos, frustration, and probably many avoidable deaths.

Abdominal, chest and head cases were carried by stretcher, while lightly wounded men walked or limped to the overcrowded beach, helped by other walking wounded. At No. 1 ACCS, seriously wounded were treated and labelled - a white label for lightly wounded, a red label for serious cases. Very soon, however, this system had to be abandoned through sheer weight of numbers. After dark, when the majority of troops had been landed, the wounded were placed on board almost anything that could float, and taken to the relative safety of those transport and troop ships still offshore. No. 1 ACCS treated over 800 casualties that day.

The work of the various medical units was not made easy by the way that the infantry had become hopelessly scattered in groups, pairs or individuals, making a thorough and systematic search for the wounded impractical. This was a feature of operations over the next week.

The diary of one field ambulance noted that 'there was great difficulty in founding systematic work as the valleys in the area were intricate and … tracks were ill-defined and difficult to recognize. Few could give directions to the location where help was required'. Battalion and regimental bearers, and doctors and their orderlies, were left to work out their own arrangements and to follow their brigades as best they could.

The lack of good maps, and therefore accurate grid references, caused havoc, as wounded could not be found and medical units were not where they were reported to be. Even at this early stage it was obvious, at least to those on shore, that the medical arrangements had gone badly wrong.

The original medical plan had assumed that all wounded would be sorted according to the severity of their wounds before leaving the beach. Manders had designated in his orders an officer to classify wounded ashore, but he cancelled the order when he ceased to be DDMS. The fully equipped hospital ships were for serious cases, the improvised ambulance carriers for less serious cases.

The overall medical plan called for four hospital ships for serious casualties and five improvised 'ambulance carriers' (or hastily fitted out transport ships) for less serious cases. But on 25 April the only hospital ship off Anzac was the *Gascon*, and at Cape Helles the *Soudan*. The other vessels did not arrive for a further 24 hours.

The hospital ship *Gascon*. Clearly marked in white with a Red Cross, these vessels were illuminated at night with green and white electric lights. (AWM H18949)

Due to the totally unexpected rush of casualties in the first few hours of the landing, this ship rapidly filled with casualties. As it had not been possible to sort them on shore, the *Gascon* received men suffering from serious wounds, as well as those with sprained ankles and cut fingers, who would normally have been placed aboard a transport or left on shore. Two transport ships that were set aside for lightly wounded cases, the *Clan MacGillivray* and the *Seang Choon*, still with contingents of troops on board, also received wounded until they too could take no more. This was one reason for the backlog of wounded that then began to accumulate on shore.

Numbers aside, the sheer lack of space at Anzac meant that field hospitals could not be established, and casualty sorting of any kind was thus impossible. Simply put, the whole scheme collapsed. The situation was just as bad at Cape Helles further south, where the 29th British Division landed. There, a witness observed that many of the casualties occurred in the boats before the landing could be effected.

These casualties were taken to warships offshore, which redirected them to the hospital ship *Soudan*, which became over crowded, thereby thwarting the original plan under which all wounded would be sent to ships specially designated to receive them, according to how serious they were.

Over the next 24 hours, members of the field ambulances gradually made contact with their regimental and battalion counterparts. One of the effects of the mix-up of units at the landing was that regimental bearers had to carry wounded all the way to the beach, instead of rendering first aid and then moving wounded a relatively short distance to safety behind the firing line, to dressing stations and field ambulances. Doctrinally the usual procedure was that the ambulance medics would continue carrying a stretcher patient from the field ambulance (behind the front line – see diagram on page 74) to the rear hospital. Unfortunately, Anzac offered little in the way of normality.

In addition to the field ambulances, No. 1 ACCS still had no shelter or protection from Ottoman artillery fire, which raked the beach from above. While there is no evidence that the enemy deliberately targeted medical units marked with a Red Cross, thoughtless siting by combatant officers often meant that legitimate targets such as stores dumps were located next to medical units, which then drew enemy fire.

Even when dug in, dressing stations and other medical treatment facilities were not immune to fire, particularly shrapnel. Many casualties were wounded again while lying on the beach. Almost all medical posts were vulnerable to small arms fire and shrapnel, and casualties among both patients and staff were frequent.

Lieutenant George Semple Bell, temporarily attached to the 6th Fd Amb, wrote: 'One of our officers, a Captain Green, was operating on a man when a shrapnel shell from Beachy Bill battery burst overhead ... and a pellet went right through his chest and Green fell into the arms of the doctor who was administering the anaesthetic'. It was worse for medics working at the very front lines, who had to continue carrying casualties up and down steep gullies under fire.

Wounded being taken off the beach by lighter to hospital and other ships standing off out of artillery range. (AWM P00166.023)

No. 1 ACCS (manned by eight officers and 77 ORs), dealt with the wounded who arrived there in hundreds from the front line and dressing stations in the gullies. This unit worked steadily throughout the day and most of the next, treating casualties from both infantry divisions.

The vast numbers of wounded forced Howse to evacuate some by boat from midday on 25 April. As part of the original medical plan the navy had positioned Beach Masters along the water's edge to act as traffic controllers for the hundreds of small boats and barges that were coming ashore, but they did not arrive until mid-morning, and there simply weren't enough of them.

There was nothing much in military history or tactical textbooks concerning the conduct of operations such as that attempted at Gallipoli. Officers found no solace in the *Manual of Combined Naval and Military Operations* (1913). Absence of precedent and lack of preparation, together with the ubiquitous workings of Murphy's Law, combined to dictate the medical response on 25 April. Nor did matters offshore proceed according to plan.

Peter Hall, an orderly with No. 2 ASH, arrived off Anzac with some of his unit aboard the *Devanah*, which was totally unprepared to receive wounded. The infantry on board were still waiting to disembark. Blankets and other medical stores had not been sterilised, as the sterilising machines had broken down. There were three RAMC doctors and 15 medics (none of whom had been trained for anything but general duties in a hospital) trying to attend to 659 wounded men, the majority of them in an awful state. Some of the wounded even offered money just to see a doctor quickly.

Another transport ship - the *Seang Bee*, which had filled up with almost 900 wounded men by Monday 26 April - could not leave the area, as her holds were still full of ammunition. The 36 inexperienced medics on board were drawn from different units, while the only two doctors aboard could not cope either mentally or physically. Sixteen loaves of bread per day were allocated to feed these 900 men. The medics spent most of their time injecting opium into casualties to ease their pain. According to one medic they went through litres of it.

Medical personnel on other ships told similar stories. One transport was asked to take 90 wounded on board. By then it was cold and raining, and these men had been towed in a small boat from ship to ship for hours seeking accommodation. Forty stretcher cases were swung on board by cargo nets swung over the side, several of whom died shortly after. One corporal placed in charge of a boatload of wounded later told Howse that he tried seven transports before he could get a ship to take his patients.

This was by no means an isolated case. Colonel Charles Ryan, an experienced Australian surgeon, later wrote that he arrived at Anzac at 0600 on 25 April. Almost at once a boatload of wounded was put on board the *Minnesota*. 'We had not made any arrangements whatever, as we did not expect to take on any wounded as the *Clan MacGillivray* was taking on wounded. I think there were fifteen to twenty cases came on board but no arrangements were made for their reception.'

Even reinforcements did little to ease matters in the first few days after the landing. Private A. Gordon, a medic, noted in his diary that on 27 April he and his section had been transferred to a troopship, where he had to look after 115 men himself, while there were only eight other orderlies to care for a further 550 wounded. He had had no sleep for three days and nights, during which he dressed, washed and fed wounded troops.

Toward evening the situation had deteriorated to such an extent that Birdwood sent a message to Hamilton suggesting a withdrawal. Admiral Cecil Thursby, who was in charge of the landing, advised Hamilton that a full-scale evacuation at night would be a complex operation that was out of the question, because many small boats had been seriously damaged or destroyed, and there was insufficient planning time. After consulting his staff and hearing grim appreciations from some Australian officers, Hamilton ordered the force ashore to dig in. The invasion force was then fully committed.

According to Howse, casualties were put on board ships that night owing to the fear that they would have to evacuate the beach at any moment. He also understood that an order was actually issued to the commander of No. 1 ACCS some time on Sunday evening that his unit was to pack and be ready to embark in two hours. Despite the difficulties, it seems that the transport of wounded from the shore to the ships was carried out effectively on 26 April, until at midnight it failed utterly, due entirely to the preparations under way at that time for an evacuation of all allied positions at Anzac.

Howse was faced with the certainty that unless special steps were taken, there would be a serious backlog of wounded on the beach, which could be kept clear of wounded only by retaining them inland or by removing them quickly offshore. He therefore concentrated on the embarkation of every wounded man as quickly as possible.

It should be noted that Birrell's scheme, which was the one being used by General Headquarters (GHQ), had no 'Plan B' should a withdrawal be ordered, nor if holding facilities could not be established inland, as was the actual situation. Howse could not have done otherwise, particularly if a withdrawal was thought imminent. Acting as his own medical embarkation officer, he obtained permission at about noon, after all available troops had landed, to clear Anzac Cove of wounded – a process that had already begun.

Much has been said about management of the flow of casualties from the beaches to ships during the last days of April. While this aspect of the medical arrangements will be analysed in greater detail below, the background to this episode can be briefly examined here. Birrell claimed he gave all the assistance he could while on board the *Arcadian* from 25 to 28 April. On 25 April he unsuccessfully tried to communicate with medical units ashore at both Anzac and Cape Helles. Both Howse (ADMS of the 1st Division) and his New Zealand counterpart, Manders (ADMS NZ&A Division) landed with the fighting troops and remained onshore, where, according to Birrell, they were out of touch with the transport ships. In any case no medical officer of any rank had access to wireless communications.

By nightfall on 25 April three Australian field ambulances and the New Zealand Fd Amb (less their tent subdivisions) had landed. These units supplied the bearer details for carrying casualties down to the beach, and also tried to provide accommodation for holding both serious and slightly wounded casualties on the peninsula. Howse established himself at the southern part of Anzac Cove (near MacLagan's Ridge) and Manders at the northern end (at Headquarters Gully or Ari Burnu – see Map 2.1 on page 26). A little over 100 kilometres away on Lemnos, No. 1 ASH (with accommodation for 400 casualties) and its staff stood idle between 25 and 28 April.

Up to 2 May Anzac casualties (killed and wounded) totalled 8364, while the British and French forces at Cape Helles and on the Asiatic shore sustained 9000.

THE FOG OF WAR

Lack of Communications

On 26 April Birrell, the DMS, asked that he or his assistant join Hamilton's HQ staff on HMS *Queen Elizabeth* to supervise evacuation, which was patently not being carried out properly. His request was refused. The lack of effective communications was a contributing factor to the inadequate treatment received by the wounded. The medical services were powerless in this respect.

There were further problems in communications. There was a chronic shortage of small boats and launches, and often the use of wireless was forbidden because of the assumed German submarine menace. Referring to Mudros Harbour just before 25 April 1915, Brigadier-General R.A. Carruthers (QMG of the ANZAC) could not communicate with other ships, as he was on a ship crowded with troops and jammed with equipment and stores. There were 120 vessels lying in the harbour, and they began to move off almost as soon as he got there. Like Birrell, he was not allowed to use the wireless and, as a launch or boat was unprocurable, he could not his transmit any orders.

The lack of effective wireless communications meant that many orders and instructions, and situation reports, had to be given manually, and carried by small boats. Manders made two attempts to get a signal to Birrell on the *Arcadian*. His first message (despatched at 1400 on 25 April) advised that he could expect about 500 wounded, and asked for another hospital ship to stand by. No reply was ever received, and it is doubtful that Birrell ever got the message.

All signals from the shore were conveyed by the wireless station close to Ari Burnu Point direct to GHQ on the *Queen Elizabeth*. Members of the general staff, who were supposed to be coordinating the evacuation of the wounded, were conspicuous by their absence. At no time did any member of this staff reply to, or act upon, the ADsMS signals.

LAST MINUTE CHANGES IN MEDICAL COMMAND

The lack of adequate consultation was not confined to members of the general staff. To compound the situation, there was at this time no DDMS at Birdwood's HQ (on the *Minnewaska*), as no one had been appointed in Manders' place when he was ordered ashore as ADMS of the NZ&A Division. Birrell was probably let down by Manders, whom he had appointed to the more important post of DDMS. But on 22 April Manders suddenly informed Birrell that, as he had been tasked by Birdwood to be ADMS of the NZ&A Division, he could not fill both positions.

In his defence, Manders had been reluctant to take on the DDMS post in the first instance due to his age (he was 55), but Howse refused the appointment when Birrell offered it to him. Manders' timing could not have been worse, as he gave his 'notice' only three days before the Gallipoli landing. As we have seen, the lack of a DDMS proved to be a serious shortcoming from 25 April to mid-May.

LACK OF HOSPITAL SHIPS

The following is a copy of a signal dated 28 April from Carruthers to Birdwood. It is quoted in full because of its later implications:

I yesterday [27 April] organised the hospital transports, put medical officers and equipment on board and despatched them to Alexandria. According to the original medical plan, no ship was supposed to leave the area for forty-eight hours. The following vessels carrying about 2,800 wounded have left. *Lutzow, Itonus, Ionian, Clan McGillivray, Seang Chun*. I have had to disorganise the field ambulances somewhat to get the medical officers and equipment … The *Hindoo* with stationary hospital equipment has never come at all. I have given all the transports orders to return as soon as possible and have told the medical officers to select and bring back any men slightly wounded who are fit to join the ranks.

HMT *Itonus* – a typical 'black ship' used to transport sick and wounded. (AWM A01802)

It was not Carruthers' responsibility to send these transport ships away, nor did he have the authority to do so. Technically this fell to Birrell. When Birdwood was advised of the chaos on board the transports, however, he immediately ordered Carruthers to put things right. The unintended consequence of this order was to dislocate AAMC units designated to accompany the disembarking troops. The situation was already complex, because the first phase of the Gallipoli offensive was an amphibious operation.

The army's responsibilities for casualties ended the moment wounded were placed on board a boat at a pier, and recommenced when those casualties were actually received on board a hospital ship (most of which were the responsibility of the army, not the navy). The navy's responsibility, according to doctrine at the time, began at the high water mark on the beaches and finished at a ship's deck.

Carruthers controlled the military aspects of medical evacuations, while his naval counterpart was the senior naval medical officer, Fleet Surgeon C.C. MacMillan. The situation got out of control partly because of the late arrival on the beaches of the naval beach parties, which landed at 1100 on 25 April. However, the fighting had been thick and fast since 0500. Naval Beach Masters tended to have a limited life span given the exposed nature of their work, and sometimes they were not replaced. There was what might seem a peculiar delineation of responsibility.

INSUFFICIENT MEDICAL PERSONNEL

Just before midnight on the evening of 25 April the *Hindoo*, which had been delayed by a storm while steaming from Egypt to Lemnos with a precious cargo of medical reinforcements (including two medical supply depots) and stores, arrived south of Anzac, just off Cape Helles. There she remained for almost three days, as no one bothered to inform senior naval or medical staff. She eventually anchored off Gaba Tepe, without unloading, on the evening of 27 April. Consequently transport ships, packed with wounded and waiting to take on desperately needed medical personnel, medicines, and medical equipment were left unprovisioned, with disastrous results.

One of the more memorable scandals of this campaign arose during this period. It concerned the *Lutzow*, a transport designated to take Australian and New Zealand wounded on the first day of the landing. Although designated as a hospital ship for 200 serious casualties and 1000 slightly wounded, there were only two men aboard her with any medical experience - a veterinary surgeon and a medical orderly. This pair was relieved after almost 80 hours of work by the arrival of two navy surgeons, who were followed almost immediately by 50 casualties from the transport *Nizam*, which at the time had an entire field ambulance on board.

The whole medical situation at Anzac between 25 April and 5 May was partly affected by the late arrival of the *Hindoo*. Had it arrived earlier, all the transports selected to carry wounded might have been adequately supplied with medical staff and equipment. In any event, neither Birrell nor the general staff oversaw the distribution of such reinforcements as there were (those of the tent subdivisions of the various ambulances, which had been left on board transport ships). It therefore fell to Carruthers to organise something. Indeed, he was the only senior administrative officer to possess a final copy of Birrell's evacuation plan, a singular advantage not shared by either Howse or Manders.

TABLE 2.1: CASUALTY FIGURES FOR ANZAC, 25-30 APRIL 1915

	KILLED IN ACTION	DIED OF WOUNDS	WOUNDED
Australians	965	161	4,114
New Zealanders	275	78	698

The Situation to 30 April

On 29 April the Royal Naval Field Ambulance of the Royal Marine Light Infantry (RMLI) landed and assisted No. 1 ACCS, providing this unit with a much-needed break, as it had been operating since the landing. By 30 April the worst was over, although the medical services were working with reduced staff due to their own casualties, and personnel being seconded to other areas. For example on 25 April alone, one field ambulance reported its own casualties as two killed, 18 wounded and four missing. Up to 30 April No. 1 ACCS had cleared more than 3000 wounded, and performed urgent orthopaedic and abdominal operations. All these necessitated anaesthetics, which were administered in nearly every instance by NCOs or by orderlies.

Medical personnel from the RAPs and the ambulances did not at first liaise with each other, and operations were entirely haphazard. The cause can be traced to the lack of instructions on how they were to keep in touch, a technique not practised during the months of training in Egypt.

Three medical NCOs at the 1st Australian Field Ambulance dressing station look on as stretcher-bearers carry a wounded Ottoman soldier. (AWM P03088.017)

After a period of trial and error, however, the RMOs arranged for their bearers to follow infantry companies, and kept for their own use two medics to assist in the RAPs. For the first few days after the landing, stretcher-bearers worked on their own initiative, some having lost contact with their own units. The 4th Fd Amb (Lieutenant-Colonel J.L. Beeston) landed on 28 April and replaced a makeshift clearing station set up on the beach near Monash Valley by the RMLI's ambulance.

In some cases the same medics who had found, retrieved, and treated casualties on shore rowed the boats. After the fire died down towards evening, they were able to get to the boats and clear the beach. The wounded were put into abandoned boats of all sizes and sea worthiness. Treatment had been basic, but effective. Medics had only simple tools – iodine and field dressings. Splints for broken limbs were improvised, the rifle being much favoured for its availability, rigidity and length, although branches and sticks were also used. As stretchers ran out because they were not returned from the transports and ambulance carriers, these too had to be improvised.

The nature of the terrain was very rugged, but once AAMC stretcher-bearers worked out routes to the beach, they made straight for No. 1 ACCS. Bearer officers, NCOs, and their squads spread over the area and responded to the call of 'Stretcher-bearer!', a job normally undertaken by bearers of the units at the front.

A typical method of organising medical units to ensure optimum performance, while allowing for rest periods, was that employed by the 3rd Fd Amb. It kept one squad in waiting, and while this squad was returning with a patient, a detail reported and another squad took its place. Two positions were therefore established: forward collecting posts near the head of Shrapnel Gully, from which the squads carried through to the beach; and detachments at halting-places halfway down the valley, where water was stored and hot drinks and food prepared.

As mentioned, the Ottoman forces generally respected the Red Cross, but there were exceptions in this early period, and some stretcher parties themselves became casualties. Certainly the hospital ships were always respected, and the enemy never fired on boats transporting wounded, although the Red Cross Flag was not always conspicuously displayed.

The deliberate shooting of wounded was rare, however, and certainly not an Ottoman monopoly, as one Digger wrote home that he witnessed a wounded Ottoman soldier try to escape, only to be shot by several Diggers. Officers and men of the medical services were equally vulnerable to both enemy and friendly fire. Some medical units lost entire stretcher-bearer parties. So-called friendly fire also claimed its victims, and naval gunfire caused a number of Australian casualties in those first days.

There were numerous, daily, acts of quiet heroism performed by members of the medical services, stretcher-bearers, or others who helped getting wounded to safety – many of these deeds were no doubt never witnessed or recorded. One of the better known individuals is Private J. Simpson [Kirkpatrick], a stretcher-bearer with the 3rd Fd Amb and his donkey. He was only one of many medics and bearers who used donkeys to convey lightly wounded soldiers between the gullies and the dressing stations. Simpson was killed by a machine-gun bullet in Shrapnel Gully on 19 May. His death has unwittingly moved the focus in current times from his colleagues who performed the same work, often continuing to do so in Palestine or on the Western Front in equally heroic circumstances.

Stretcher-bearers of the 1st Australian Field Ambulance about 2 May. The unit's adjutant, Major Edward Sutherland-Stokes, is reading divisional orders. (AWM C02148)

AN INTERLUDE

After the critical shortage of medical personnel passed, the 2nd and 3rd LH Fd Ambs (Lieutenant-Colonels H.K. Bean and Rupert Downes) landed on 12 May. They did not stay long, however, as in an attempt to save water on the peninsula, they were redeployed to Lemnos on 26 June. On 13 May all shipping sailed for Lemnos due to a submarine scare. As will be seen, the presence or rumour of submarines off the peninsula was a serious inconvenience to the allies, particularly the medical authorities who tried to ensure adequate evacuation procedures for the wounded and sick.

Toward the end of May the situation improved marginally, as military arrangements settled, definite front lines were established, and there were fewer battle casualties. Wells were sunk, medical units dug in, housekeeping became the norm, small piers were built, and most importantly medical stores were landed. Death and uncertainty, however, remained.

Australian positions were suddenly and heavily shelled in the very early hours of 19 May, and troops stood to in their trenches. Minutes later they were rushed by the enemy. The attackers failed, and were repulsed with heavy losses – their casualties were in some cases as high as 50 percent due to particularly effective Australian machine-gun fire. These corpses added to the dead of both sides, who had lain in rotting heaps in front of the trenches for some time. On

20 May, two Ottoman medical officers with Red Crescent (the Islamic equivalent of the Red Cross) flags approached Pope's Hill (see Map 2.1 on page 26), and two Australian medical officers went to meet them. The enemy requested an armistice to bury their dead and collect their wounded.

The armistice, which was granted from 0730 to 1630 on Monday 24 May, had good health reasons behind it. The corpses were not only 'a nauseating source of discomfort to the defenders', but were a breeding place for blowflies. The truce also provided an opportunity for the Anzacs to exchange their grim army biscuits for Turkish rye bread, and in some cases to glean additional munitions of a more deadly nature.

Some 3000 dead Ottoman soldiers were buried where they lay, removing what had been a serious cause of loss of morale among enemy troops manning trenches there. Any Ottoman rifles found by the Australians had their bolts removed and were handed to the enemy. As neither Birdwood nor his Ottoman counterpart Esat Pasha had sufficient troops to continue aggressive fighting, a lull fell over the battlefield.

To show that things were little better in the British sector of the peninsula, something can be said briefly about the attack on the small village of Krithia near the southern tip of the peninsula on 6 May, in which the 2nd Brigade (which had just been reinforced with 732 men after its earlier losses during the landing), the New Zealand Brigade, and their field ambulances participated. This attack was the culmination of two days of battle, in which both British and French troops failed to seize the Achi Baba feature. Krithia lay to the north of Achi Baba on an area of flat ground interspersed with small folds, which the Ottoman soldiers used to maximum effect to site their machine-guns.

None of the officers were properly briefed, their unprepared men had to deploy while still eating their dinner, and the assaults were conducted in full daylight. The subsequent attacks and counter-attacks caused heavy casualties. The 2nd Brigade lost 75 percent of its original strength of 3885 men and the New Zealand Brigade, which suffered over 835 casualties, had its effective strength reduced to 268 men. Only two if its officers remained unwounded. Many casualties lay in the open until they could be retrieved under cover of darkness. Most suffered serious abdominal wounds from machine-gun fire. Two-man stretcher parties had a carrying distance of up to three kilometres.

There were parallels with the Australian and New Zealand experience at Anzac Cove. First, the British medical officer in charge of this action was told about it only the afternoon before, and had little opportunity to coordinate his medical units with those of the Anzacs. Subsequently the officer commanding the 2nd Fd Amb received no instructions. The DMS (Birrell) again was absent. The same problem of a shortage of stretchers was experienced. During and after the Krithia operation there was a delay of up to five days before most of the serious casualties were treated. Australian stretcher-bearers suffered heavy casualties.

CHAPTER 3:

From the August Offensive to the Evacuation

There was a significant (and to some extent avoidable) repetition of the mistakes of the landing during the major offensive of 6 to 13 August. By then, however, and certainly by the final withdrawal from the peninsula in mid-December 1915, senior AIF medical officers were more forceful in insisting on being fully briefed before major operations.

The period between May and August was punctuated by relatively small-scale skirmishes, probes and reconnaissance patrols, and battle casualty figures began to be overtaken by the number of soldiers falling sick. By the middle of August the condition of the men was awful. They are often described as 'thin, haggard, weak as kittens, and covered with suppurating sores'. Many were also suffering from dysentery.

The daily sick parade reports were beginning to record an accelerating incidence of sickness, chiefly diarrhoea and dysentery. In the case of one battalion on 27 August, 180 men out of a total strength of 220 appeared on sick parade. Their opponents were also beginning to be ravaged by typhus. The combat effectiveness of units on both sides plummeted.

According to the Turkish official history of the campaign, in operations from 25 April to 1 July 1915, the ratio of wounded to sick men in the Ottoman hospital system was about 24:1 (only 2358 sick for the period April, May and June 1915). It is unclear why the ratio of wounded to sick was so lopsided. The Ottoman forces had abundant supplies of fresh water, adequate food and (something not yet in place in the AIF) rest camps out of enemy artillery firing range behind the lines. As the campaign wore on, however, the peninsula became very crowded, sanitary conditions deteriorated, and the enemy ran short of imported medicines.

Chronic ill-health among the allies due to disease had two immediate consequences. First, it cut further the already reduced manpower of the medical services. By late September there was a shortage of 22 medical officers in the 1st Division alone. Second, sick men had to be accommodated somewhere, and there were frequent occasions when heavy shelling, submarine activity or storms caused a serious backlog of casualties at both field ambulances and dressing stations on Gallipoli.

QUESTIONS OF ADMINISTRATION

In Egypt, the medical situation was characterised by improvisation, lack of staff, and the staggering loss to the field army of thousands of mildly sick or slightly wounded troops being evacuated to Britain and Australia. These should have been treated in Egypt or Malta, and returned to the fighting.

Ford made neither calculations of casualty figures, nor provision for them, before the landing. Instead, he was content to wait until casualties were landed in Egypt. The *Gascon* arrived in Alexandria with 48 hours' notice, followed shortly thereafter by the five transport ships (and their 2849 casualties) despatched with no prior notice from Anzac by Carruthers.

The lack of preparation also meant that these transport ships, once emptied of their human cargo, sailed back to Gallipoli without any attempt being made to clean or refurbish them with medical stores, so causing a severe drain on the limited medical resources on Gallipoli when they arrived there. Until 9 May Australian and New Zealand troops accounted for 75 percent of the 7884 casualties who arrived in Egypt.

Matters were little better elsewhere. For months after April the medical arrangements on Lemnos continued to be ignored. It was a victim of the continued reluctance on the part of the GHQ to upgrade the harbour at Mudros to an advanced expeditionary base. This situation may be partly explained by the unfounded optimism of Hamilton and his staff, who believed that a breakthrough on the peninsula was still within their grasp. This was despite the fact that by mid-May the navy had made the harbour its official administrative base.

No attempts were made at Mudros to drill for water on a scale large enough to cater for hospitals of any size. Because of this, No. 19 British General Hospital, which arrived on 24 May from Britain, had to be redeployed to Alexandria. Lemnos was the closest Australian nurses came to serving at the Gallipoli front, and about 100 nurses served there in very rough conditions between August 1915 and February 1916.

After the arrival on Lemnos of Major-General Sir E.A. Altham, the Inspector-General of Communications, in mid-July, the harbour there began to take on the appearance of a proper base, with piers, roads, and hospital sites constructed. Roads meant motor ambulances, and the first of the large Australian fleet of motor ambulances already operating in Egypt were sent over, making life much easier for both patients and medical staff.

Babtie's preparations, however, were still substantially incomplete by the time of the next large scale military operation on Gallipoli - the August Offensive. This was part of a major attempt by the allies to end the stalemate on the peninsula, and to secure substantial territorial gains.

Medical reinforcements did not land at Mudros Harbour until 7 August. No. 3 AGH, without its equipment, was sent to Mudros, as were Nos. 1 and 3 Canadian Stationary Hospitals (which arrived at Mudros on 16 August). At the beginning of August Nos. 1 and 2 ASHs were fully deployed, but their equipment was either 'lost' or on ships still at sea. Part of the medical arrangements for August included greater utilisation of the small island of Imbros, some 19 kilometres from Anzac, which straddled the sea route between Gallipoli and Lemnos.

Despite Porter's approach to the general staff at this time, he could obtain little information about the proposed battle, apart from the intimation that there would be an attack at Gallipoli on 6 August. Porter finally managed to obtain a plan of the operations to ascertain what arrangements had been made for the wounded. After reviewing these, he decided they were grossly inadequate in terms of the necessary hospital ships allocated.

THE AUGUST OFFENSIVE

Hamilton's attempt to break the deadlock that had developed since April comprised a series of set piece attacks from Cape Helles in the south to Suvla Bay in the northern part of the peninsula. While preparations for the August Offensive had been underway since 13 July, senior RAMC and AAMC officers were not privy to the plan until the very eve of the offensive, 6 August.

In his sector, Birdwood developed a plan using a classic pincer manoeuvre. This plan basically comprised a surprise night attack against the heights of the Sari Bair feature and its summit, Hill 971. The key objective was the high ground that overlooked the Anzac perimeter. Seizing both Hill 971 and Battleship Hill would put the Ottoman forces at a tactical disadvantage, and force them to yield ground.

There were to be diversions or feints by the 1st Division (at Lone Pine) and by the NZ&A Division (on The Nek), assisted by British troops landed at Cape Helles. (See Map 3.2 on page 45). The offensive was a complete disaster, and for both sides these attacks and counter-attacks were exceptionally bloody.

The allied offensive began on the afternoon of Friday 6 August with attacks at Cape Helles and Lone Pine. Three battalions of mainly sick men attacked the heavily fortified Lone Pine position. The fighting, some of most intense in the campaign, continued to see-saw over the next few days, during which the enemy sustained disproportionately higher casualties.

While the allies clung to Lone Pine, and briefly captured the strategically important heights of Chunuk Bair, the latter position was retaken in a dawn attack on 10 August, commanded by Lieutenant-Colonel Mustafa Kemal. Part of this operation was the infamous charge by men of the 8th and 10th Light Horse Regiments on the feature called The Nek, with no success, but many casualties.

Once more the medical and evacuation systems were simply overwhelmed. Little had been learned, and despite the best efforts of some planners many of the same mistakes (medical, logistical and tactical) were repeated.

The area occupied by the 1st Division was expected to bear the heaviest casualties, and Howse took steps to avoid a repetition of the April fiasco. Also, Colonel A.E.C. Keble, the ADMS, MEF arrived on 5 August to act as Medical Control Officer. Lieutenant-Colonel John Corbin of No. 1 ACCS was made Medical Embarkation Officer, and several RAMC officers were seconded to assist with sorting or triaging casualties. Soldiers with minor wounds were sent to Mudros, and those seriously wounded were evacuated by ship direct to Egypt. Even so, the scale of the attack, and its sheer complexity, again largely neutralised these measures.

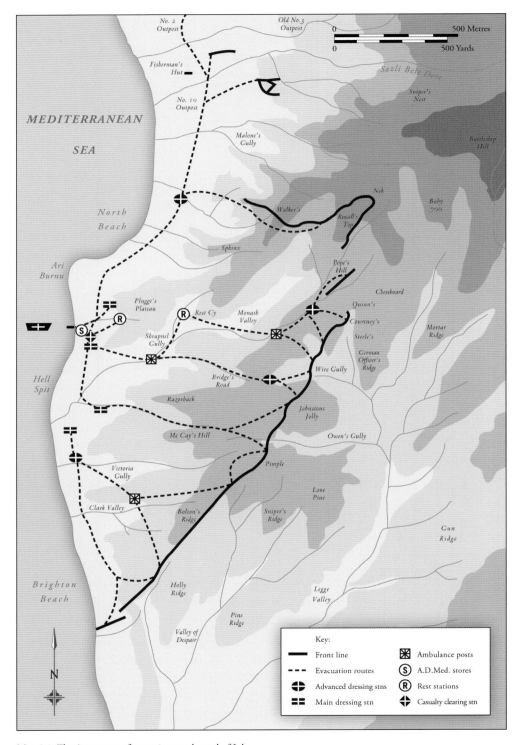

Map 3.1. The Anzac area of operations at the end of July.

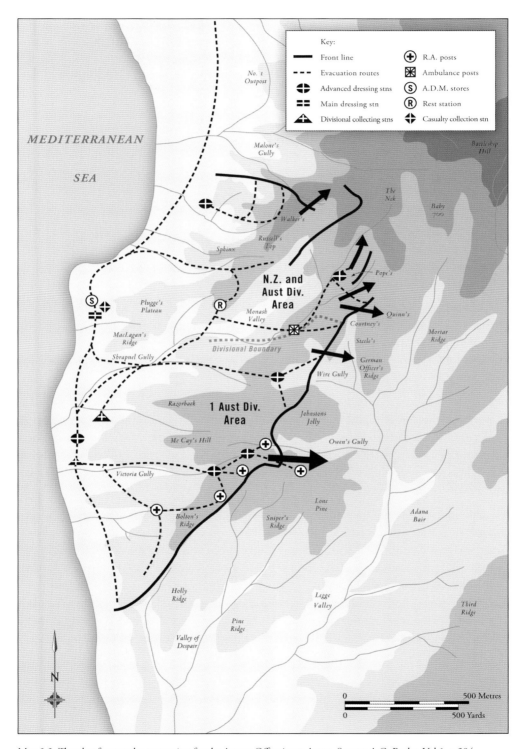

Map 3.2. The plan for casualty evacuation for the August Offensive at Anzac. Source: A.G. Butler, Vol.1, p.294.

In the NZ&A Division's sector, Manders proposed a detailed plan, using accurate copies of maps taken from Ottoman prisoners. He presented these 1:20,000 scale maps (a vast improvement on the 1:40,000 scale maps used in April) on the afternoon of 6 August. Manders had at his disposal the 1st and 3rd LH Fd Ambs and the 4th Fd Amb. In addition he had his own New Zealand Fd Amb and part of the New Zealand Mounted Fd Amb and an Indian field ambulance, while Nos. 13 and 16 British CCSs provided triaging and treating facilities.

There was no preliminary naval bombardment, as there had been in April, to forewarn the enemy of an imminent attack. But other signs must have been noted by the enemy, particularly the hospital ships that lay off Anzac Cove and Cape Helles.

Some mistakes were repeated, with the same disastrous consequences. In the first hurried rush to evacuate wounded, most of the available stretchers ended up at Mudros. Consequently there were few left for the hundreds of cases waiting to be brought to the beaches. There were more hospital ships this time, and better on board preparation for surgical procedures. There were, however, other features present during this offensive that were absent in April: disease and sickness.

By August every Australian and New Zealand medical unit was under-strength, and inefficient administrative procedures meant that some hospital ships and carriers were still undermanned. Babtie recognised this, but was largely helpless because of a lack of readily available trained personnel to deploy to these vessels. At the front, medical officers marshalled their resources as best they could.

On Friday 6 August the RMO of the 14th Battalion had 12 stretcher-bearers, a battalion corporal medical orderly, and five other medics, but he only had six spare stretchers. His preparations included sandbags filled with dressings, in addition to a sandbag of dressings wrapped up in each stretcher. He ordered his bearers to carry back no wounded during the night advance, only to bandage them and leave them on the track. Medics and bearers continued to advance until the battalion reached its destination.

As early as 0600 the first of the field ambulances began sending urgent appeals for reinforcements, although in some instances several days passed before additional staff arrived on the peninsula. Every doctor, medic and bearer worked non-stop. In isolated areas on the slopes, in gullies and ravines, wherever wounded had grouped together, lone medical officers did their best, often by the dim light of a hurricane lamp. By 8 August an improvised collecting station formed by men of the 1st Fd Amb could only muster one doctor and 35 medics. Together they handled a continuous stream of casualties, and in 24 hours dealt with 1500 wounded. Earlier that day the same bearers had also carried and treated casualties from an attack on Holly Ridge.

The 1st LH Fd Amb followed the troops attacking Chailak Dere, and evacuated wounded to the beach as it went. Cooperative attempts to form relay posts from the front, down through the gullies to the beach, soon proved unworkable. A New Zealand ambulance that established a dressing station below the light horse unit was shelled and had to move, while casualties were accumulating so fast they could not be evacuated. It was all that medical units could do to carry out first aid.

The next day (9 August), the 1st LH Fd Amb also had to call for reinforcements. A Welsh ambulance unit further down the gully, which had acted as a relay post, could not cope with the rush and collapsed, forcing the light horse bearers to carry wounded all the way to the beach. At times even cooks were called on to assist in carrying wounded on stretchers. The night attacks and the unfamiliar terrain contributed to the confusion.

The stress for some became unbearable and they sought to leave the field. Officers did not have to resort to the self-inflicted wounds of the ordinary soldier to escape. At a time when every available man was needed, the contempt for the few who fled is evident in a diary entry by Beeston: 'The number of officers clearing out is not commendable. One cannot wonder at the men squibbing it, one is more and more surprised at officers in whom we would have placed every confidence before the War and they are so barefaced about it too'.

The carefully husbanded stocks of medical supplies held by RMOs, dressing stations, and field ambulances began to run low. Unlike the April disaster, there were adequate medical stores on depot ships just offshore, but the difficulty was getting appropriate requisition orders to the ships, having these processed, and then finding the men to bring stores back to where they were needed. All this took time, something in very short supply for the medical services during this period.

Fortunately during this offensive all sub-units of the field ambulances were used, including their tent subdivisions. Men from these sections were responsible for dressing wounds, splinting, and assisting in operations. In August more medical manpower was theoretically available, but this was offset by units being undermanned due to death, injury or sickness among the medics and bearers themselves.

Units like No. 1 ACCS on the beach were hard pressed. In addition to caring for wounded from its own area, it received all the British walking wounded from the disastrous Suvla Bay fighting further north. They could not be evacuated owing to transport difficulties there. In just over two days No. 1 ACCS treated approximately 5000 men.

The lot of the wounded was made worse because many of them fought wearing only the bare essentials (hat, boots and improvised shorts), as a concession to the daytime heat. Therefore, a badly wounded man who could not walk might have to lie half-naked all through the night, in bitter cold.

At various stages of the offensive, those wounded who did reach the piers where the medical barges came alongside found that the least wounded were often evacuated first. A senior New Zealand officer noted that the 'lack of facilities for evacuating wounded was as pronounced as at the landing'. He also observed that when a flotilla of Red Cross barges reached the beach, the walking wounded would crowd onto the pier in anticipation of getting off, leaving helpless men on the beach.

Medical staff had to keep a close watch to ensure that serious cases went to the hospital ships, while the less serious ones were directed to hospital carriers destined for Lemnos. No. 1 ACCS was faced with the same difficulties on the beach as in April, particularly a shortage of small boats and sea transport.

Nos. 13 and 16 British CCSs, designated as reinforcements, landed under extremely adverse circumstances, very late, having been sent by mistake to Suvla Bay instead of Anzac. Subsequently, they were unable to prepare themselves properly. There ensued utter chaos on the left flank of the 1st Division's sector, and at Keble's request Corbin went there on 12 August with extra medical officers, and tried to help the RAMC units. The conditions they met were appalling.

The war diary of No. 1 ACCS for 15 and 23 August suggests why. The commander of No. 13 British CCS (Colonel McNaught) was seriously ill, and his unit had shelter only adequate for fair weather – bearing in mind the time of year. In the case of No. 16 British CCS, its evacuation pier was under rifle fire, and it had been set up in the 'dry' bed of a then full-flowing stream. Fetherston also mentions this bungle, and suggests that this unit collapsed from 'nervousness and ignorance', not from over work.

Scenes strikingly reminiscent of the original landing were re-enacted in the NZ&A Division's sector, where the objective was the heights of Chunuk Bair. Wounded lay and died in the overcrowded No. 1 ACCS on the beach. Shelling during the day made evacuation impossible, and the numbers of wounded grew. Manders, who worked so hard to make sure that this battle would not see the tragedy of the wounded at the landing repeated, knew all his medical resources were exhausted. The next day he was killed.

Strategically, nothing was gained in this sector. On this flank, Manders' units were later joined by sections of the 31st and 39th British Fd Ambs, which employed trained ambulance dogs to find casualties. Manders' death may have contributed to problems in the medical arrangements at Chunuk Bair, which deteriorated more rapidly than those of the 1st Division further south, where medical procedures were overseen by the indefatigable Howse.

The medical aid post at the base of Quinn's and Pope's Posts. (AWM A02692)

Units of the 1st Division were engaged in a massive diversion along the front line, stretching from Quinn's Post in the north to Lone Pine in the south (see Map 3.2 on page 45). The affiliated medical units of the 1st Division under Howse consisted of the 2nd and 3rd Fd Ambs. The casualties were appalling. The attack on and about Lone Pine decimated the battalions thrown into this desperate battle. A similarly heroic assault on The Nek was just as devastating. Only 31 percent of the two regiments of the 3rd Light Horse Brigade that were engaged (the 8th and 10th Light Horse Regiments) returned unwounded.

Not only were there insufficient medics, no special provision had been made for these diversionary attacks, as no one on the general staff had taken the trouble to inform Birrell. Originally Howse had been designated the medical 'controller' of the beach for the August attack. However, on the strength of a report he sent to Birrell, in which he expressed his dissatisfaction with the medical arrangements, he was relieved by Keble, which allowed Howse to concentrate on medical arrangements for the 1st Division.

To summarise, despite better planning the August Offensive had much in common with everything that went wrong in April, although in August there was at least an awareness of the implications of large numbers of casualties for the Lines of Communication. Casualties among the medical services alone were of the order of 15 percent.

What set the August actions apart were the traffic jams caused by large number of reinforcements and munitions being forced up defiles (such as at Aghyl Dere and Chailak Dere on the evening of 8 August). These defiles were so narrow they forced men to walk in single file, while at the same time large numbers of wounded were trying to get back down along the same route to the beaches and comparative safety. Stretcher-bearers had no right of way. Added to this were the blistering heat of the day and the extreme cold of the evenings – many badly wounded men died from exposure where they lay.

The medical arrangements for evacuation were seriously disorganised, because the two British CCSs that were sent to help did not arrive on 6 August, and could not be found. Apparently the captain of their ship was ordered to disembark both units at Anzac if he arrived there before dark. He duly arrived, but as he was unable to contact anyone on the beach, he proceeded north to Suvla Bay under contingency orders. Only when they arrived there did the naval traffic officer receive a cable ordering the two British CCSs back to Anzac. This delay cost lives.

By 8 August the medical services were on the brink of exhaustion – on that night over 1000 men lay exposed on the beaches waiting evacuation. The night before, the only hospital ship off Anzac, the packed *Sicila*, was already refusing to take wounded. Some small boats, which could not find a ship to take their wounded, returned to the shore, only to be shelled by the Ottoman artillery, which believed they carried reinforcements. Medical reinforcements, in the form of the tent subdivisions of six Australian and New Zealand field ambulances, arrived on 11 August, but after the worst was over. By 14 August, there were sufficient boats to clear the wounded from Gallipoli.

The preparations made for the August Offensive by the AAMC, although adequate in themselves for dealing with troop operations in the Anzac sector, were seriously disrupted by the relatively large number of casualties and by lack of communication (and insufficient notice) from Hamilton's GHQ. Of the 51,867 casualties, sick and wounded, who left the peninsula between 7 August and 8 September, 23,686 (45.6 percent) were from the Anzac front.

POST-SCRIPT TO THE AUGUST PERIOD

It is easy to overlook the importance of the weather, not only during the campaign itself, but also as a key planning consideration for the medical services. Like the terrain, the weather affected such things as accommodation on the peninsula and exposure, and the availability or otherwise of hospital ships, which was dictated by good weather. Troops who landed in April were subjected to very hot weather at first, together with the associated medical and sanitary problems the heat inevitably brought with it – particularly flies.

From October the weather moved to the other extreme, and for most Australians it was the first time that they had seen snow. The novelty, however, soon wore off. By November gales strewed the beaches with wreckage – tugs, steamboats, flotsam and corpses. In one particularly bleak week a blizzard swept down from the north-east, causing appalling suffering to both sides. On the night of 28 November, when the blizzard was at its worst, floods of icy water washed away the parapets of many enemy trenches. Hundreds of men either drowned or died of exposure.

Offshore, after the worst of the fighting was over, the wounded were better cared for than soldiers who were wounded or sick in April, or even at the beginning of August. For example, aboard the *Caledonian*, on which about 1000 mainly sick men were placed, medical officers noted that there was not nearly such a rush, and the men were not in such a frightful condition. The wounded brought on board also had their wounds better dressed ashore. Soldiers were competently cared for when the medical staff at Anzac were adequately staffed and prepared, had the time to perform their tasks, and were not overwhelmed by sudden rushes of huge numbers of casualties from infantry 'stunts'.

THE FINAL EVACUATION – DECEMBER 1915

By October the Ottoman forces on Gallipoli were at their maximum strength, when 5500 officers and 310,000 men were listed on the rolls of the *5th Army*. The campaign had been a manifest failure. The fate of the MEF was sealed when Kitchener, Minister of War and one of the initial supporters of the landing, visited the Dardanelles on 10 October. On 22 November he recommended to the British Cabinet that all British and allied forces on Gallipoli be withdrawn.

Hamilton was relieved of his command on 16 October, once the August Offensive had been fully assessed by the War Office, and replaced by General Sir Charles Monro, an experienced commander from the Western Front. After a lightning one-day reconnaissance of all three fronts on the peninsula, Monro made his own appreciation of the situation. Preparation of plans for a full evacuation began almost immediately.

Two different schemes were submitted. The first called for a phased withdrawal from position to position on the peninsula. The second, submitted by Godley, recommended that every man surplus to the barest minimum necessary to hold the front should be removed from the front line, and evacuated direct to the sea over two nights. Fortunately for the medical services the second plan was adopted.

Secrecy was vital, and this was ensured by reducing the garrison over the winter months, ostensibly to allow rest and recreation for troops who had been on the peninsula since April. As we shall see, this length of time without relief from the constant dangers, privations and stress of fighting contributed significantly to the deteriorating mental and physical health of the Diggers.

CONFIDENTIAL

MEDITARRANEAN EXPEDITIONARY FORCE

CIRCULAR MEMORANDUM FOR MEDICAL OFFICERS AND NURSES IN HOSPTAL SHIPS AND AMBULANCE CARRIERS

IT HAS BEEN BROUGHT TO THE NOTICE OF SIR IAN HAMILTON THAT, HERE AND THERE, ON HOSPITAL SHIPS AND AMBULANCE CARRIERS, MEDICAL OFFICERS AND NURSES HAVE ALLOWED THEMSELVES TO BECOME TOO SERIOUSLY IMPRESSED BY THE STORIES OF YOUNG OFFICERS AND MEN WHO HAVE COME ON BOARD SICK OR WOUNDED. IT IS NATURAL, UNDER THE CONDITIONS, THAT THESE TALES SHOULD BE OVER-COLOURED, IT IS NATURAL ALSO THAT CONTACT WITH SO MUCH SUFFERING SHOULD INCLINE THE LISTENERS TO SYMPATHY, BUT IT IS CERTAIN ALSO THAT , WHETHER FROM THE STANDPOINT OF THE INDIVIDUAL SICK OR OF THE MILITARY OPERATIONS AS A WHOLE, SUCH ENERVATING INFLUENCES SHOULD BE RESISTED.

ALL GRADES AND DEGREES OF THE MEDICAL STAFF MUST MAKE IT A POINT OF PROFESSIONAL HONOUR TO MAINTAIN A HEARTY TONE OF OPTIMISM TO RAISE RATHER THAN LOWER THE CONFIDENCE AND COURAGE OF THE FIGHTING MEN WHO HAVE BEEN TEMPORARILY COMMITTED TO THEIR CHARGE...LET MEDICAL OFFICERS AND NURSES ON HOSPITAL SHIPS AND AMBULANCE CARRIERS SEE TO IT THEN THAT, UNDER ALL TRIALS, THEY SURROUND THEIR SICK AND WOUNDED WITH AN ATMOSPHERE OF ENTHUSIASM AND OF INVINCIBLE HOPE.

WAR OFFICE, 5TH OCTOBER 1915

The evacuation must rank as one of the most successfully concealed operations in military history. Given that camps and hospitals might have harboured Ottoman and German spies (often Greek labourers), its success was even more remarkable. It is almost incredible that such a secret should be so well kept, when even medical officers, traditionally 'on the outer', were aware of a proposed December evacuation. The enemy, too, was suspicious. One German officer wrote after the war that rumours and suggestions that the allies were going to evacuate Gallipoli 'swarmed' around the Ottoman lines.

Two features set the final evacuation apart from the landing eight months earlier. First, the planning was meticulous, and left little to chance. Second, there was an almost universal lack of optimism concerning its success. Monro expected fully one-third of his force to become casualties. On 4 November even before he arrived on his tour of inspection of Gallipoli, Kitchener instructed Birdwood (who opposed the idea) to prepare an evacuation plan. Birdwood's planning for both the April landing and the August Offensive had been less than competent, so it fell to his able chief-of-staff, Brudenell White to design and implement the withdrawal plan.

The first real intimation to the Australian medical services that something was afoot came on 19 November, when the British ADMS at Mudros held a conference of the commanding officers of all the medical units on Lemnos. According to the commanding officer of the 2nd Fd Amb, they discussed the 'accommodation of a large number of wounded from Gallipoli in connection, so it is rumoured, with the proposed evacuation of the Peninsula'.

A week later, on 26 November, Birdwood officially told Sutton, the acting DDMS, ANZAC, that the garrison at Anzac was to be reduced. Sutton immediately suggested that several medical units be evacuated. These included Nos. 13 and 16 British CCSs (after they cleared their wounded), and all the field ambulances of the 54th British Division and the 2nd Division. Actually, however, No. 13 British CCS remained until the end. He also suggested the immediate evacuation of all sick and any other men who could be spared. The 2nd LH Fd Amb was warned for imminent transfer to Mudros. Birdwood told Sutton to put all these units on standby, but not to issue any written orders for their removal.

Secrecy remained paramount, so the outside world, including senior British medical authorities in Egypt, could not yet be informed. Howse sent a letter (dated 12 December 1915) by hand to Surgeon-General William Bedford in Cairo, asking for his assistance in maintaining a good supply of hospital ships so that in the event of an evacuation, Howse would not be forced to leave any sick or wounded at Anzac.

There was a conference on the morning of 14 December with the general staff and other officers, including Howse, and the next day *Army Corps Order No. 21* was issued, which gave details of the evacuation arrangements. The day was spent building up caches of stores, such as food, water, candles, oil and fuel. Two medical units were detailed to remain. Howse instructed the officer commanding No. 1 ACCS to continue taking in supplies until it and No. 13 British CCS had sufficient for a total of 1200 patients for 30 days. There was to be no repeat of what occurred on 25 April.

The liner *Mauretania* before being converted to a hospital ship. Her size reflects the demands of the growing casualty lists. (Source: http://en.wikipedia.org/wiki/RMS_Mauretania_1906)

As the campaign drew to a close after eight long months, hospital ships were still in short supply. This was soon corrected, but it was important not to alert the enemy by having unusually large numbers of these ships off Gallipoli. At this time only the *Devanha* – already crowded with sick – was standing on station. However the harbour of Mudros saw the beginnings of an armada being assembled. Instead of two or three small hospital ships waiting there, the largest passenger liners afloat at the time, the *Britannic*, the *Aquitania* (these two ships alone took almost 6000 wounded and sick on their first trip from Mudros Harbour), the *Mauretania* and the *Franconia*, had been pressed into service as hospital ships.

While the medical component of the army was small compared with the infantry and some of the other logistics services, it still had a relatively large number of units, all of which had to be considered in the evacuation. On returning to Gallipoli, Howse issued his instructions on 10 December.

Units were to evacuate their patients to either No. 1 ACCS or No. 13 British CCS, then pack their equipment unostentatiously, under tents as far as possible, which were to be left standing. They were to leave a few of their men to move about their camp sites and maintain signs of occupation. By the next day all the equipment of the Australian and New Zealand medical units had been put aboard transports – no mean achievement.

Then, on the evening of 11 December orders were received to evacuate all sick and wounded to No. 1 ACCS by 0800 the next day. There were exemptions, however, including men suffering from scarlet fever or infectious diseases, and men with self-inflicted wounds. These orders were followed by more detailed instructions the next day, including orders to convey all alcohol to No. 1 ACCS – although not all of it arrived. Casualties were not to be admitted to field ambulances, but passed directly to No. 1 ACCS.

Over the next few days all valuable medical equipment, such as machinery, surgical instruments, and drugs, was cleared to the beach under the direct supervision of Howse. Troops embarking were to carry one day's rations and a full water bottle. Water, food, ordinary dressings, stretchers, and blankets were left in all dressing stations, just in case.

Howse left Anzac on the evening of 18 December after appointing Lieutenant-Colonel R.D. Campbell, commanding No. 1 ACCS, to remain as Senior Medical Officer – Anzac, with instructions to evacuate or hold the remaining two clearing stations in accordance with the numbers of casualties reported. No. 1 ACCS was to stay until last, as it was the most sheltered and the best equipped. To it, the first complete medical unit to land on Gallipoli, was given the honour of embarking last.

Its members were detailed to care for the wounded should disaster overtake the rearguard. Medics and bearers were each equipped with a surgical haversack containing field dressings and morphine The dressing stations were left equipped with the necessary instruments, so that if the enemy were not fooled and attacked in force, the wounded could be tended by men of their own medical services. It was hoped that the enemy might allow lifeboats from the hospital ships to approach the shore to evacuate any seriously wounded.

Early on Monday 20 December, both clearing stations left the beaches to board the *Dongola*, and disembarked at Lemnos. Casualties during the final night of the evacuation totalled three men who were hit by stray bullets. The last Australian casualties in hospitals on Lemnos were not evacuated until early January.

There is no doubt that the final evacuation from Gallipoli was a masterly achievement of elaborate staff work, organised in minute detail, which planned for almost every contingency. It was a far cry from the rushed and vague preparations that characterised the initial landing in April.

Close coordination between front-line units and base hospitals in Cairo, and an increasingly efficient use of manpower, became hallmarks of AAMC units and personnel on the peninsula. As with the medical services of the other Dominions, theirs was a steep learning curve. In both periods these were overshadowed, and sometimes mismanaged, by a vast imperial military medical bureaucracy. This was always a risk in coalition operations.

CHAPTER 4:

Keeping Soldiers Alive

As we have seen, until the end of August the medical arrangements on Gallipoli were flawed and mainly reactive. Factors contributing to this state of affairs were extremes of weather, terrain, lack of water, and the distances between front-line medical units and base hospitals. The implications for surgery and the lack of orderly and regular evacuation from Gallipoli will be readily appreciated.

GETTING THE WOUNDED TO MEDICAL AID

Almost throughout the Gallipoli campaign, AAMC units were badly understaffed, a situation that became worse as disease spread on the peninsula. There was also the perennial problem of units along the Lines of Communications being overwhelmed by battle casualties. This occurred on Gallipoli, Lemnos and in Egypt, as we shall see.

For example, almost as soon as the 3rd LH Fd Amb opened as a temporary 50-bed hospital at Mudros in June, 83 British wounded arrived from Cape Helles. Efforts to supplement stores were unsuccessful. Two months later on Gallipoli, the same unit recorded that it treated 884 patients in hospital, even though it had to wait weeks before obtaining much needed equipment, while cooking and eating utensils were only procured shortly before it closed.

Sometimes a soldier waited for days before receiving care. Endurance, therefore, was an important requirement for the Diggers, a trait observed along with the Australian 'devil-may-care' attitude: 'One man [who] had both legs & one arm broken, two abdominal wounds, one thru chest & one in the neck – he asked me if I thought his leg was broken'.

There is also the case of Private Frank Clune of the 16th Battalion, who was wounded in both legs. After meeting two of his mates who were also wounded, they hid behind a bush. One volunteered to bandage Clune's leg, from which blood was oozing, and the other loaded his rifle, which he had been using as a crutch. He stayed with them all day and 'just sniped Turks in between times'. After dark some stretcher-bearers found them, and took them to a dressing station.

FIRST AID

Unfortunately for both casualties and medical staff on Gallipoli, all transport was by stretcher, foot, or by donkey – none of which improved the condition of the casualty. In many cases they had to face a long wait on the beach and a rough boat ride when being taken to a ship. This is not to suggest that the comfort of the wounded was ignored, but short of administering morphine, there was little capacity to ease a wounded man's condition. Improvisation was always in evidence, and when a soldier was suffering from fractured bones, limbs were often immobilised using sandbags and coats while he was being carried by stretcher. Some stretchers were even fitted with cradles to sling a leg.

An important consideration in treating sick and wounded soldiers was the need to return them to the trenches or their units as soon as possible. The medical officers on the peninsula played a very important part in determining who would be evacuated and who could be sent back to their units (sometimes after being held at a medical facility on Gallipoli for several days).

Such was the camaraderie of the troops that men remained too long in their dugouts before reporting sick. It was then too late to do anything other than to evacuate them from Anzac, the very thing these Diggers had tried to avoid. After August, disease relieved doctors of this responsibility, necessitating massive reinforcements, and ultimately withdrawal from the Dardanelles.

Throughout the campaign, conditions on Gallipoli dictated what treatment could or could not be given to soldiers. This was particularly true of surgery, most of which was carried out on hospital ships or in the better equipped hospitals in Mudros, Alexandria or Cairo.

TOOLS OF THE TRADE

AIF Shell dressing, supplied to all troops, it was often an effective first aid measure to control bleeding. (AWM REL34451)

At the front, treatment was of the most basic kind. After reaching a casualty, stretcher-bearers were trained to stop any bleeding first, then take the casualty to safety, after which broken bones were splinted and the man carried to the next stage in the long evacuation chain.

The standard method used to control bleeding was the application of a small compressed sterile bandage, which every soldier carried. This was known as the first field dressing. Unfortunately they were sometimes of indifferent quality, and there is no doubt some Australian firms supplied sub-standard products. As we shall see, profiteering by Australian contractors extended to other medical items.

Where severe bleeding was involved, a tourniquet was used. This was usually a thin strip of material, string or rubber, placed around a limb and, with the aid of a stick, twisted and locked in position, stopping the flow of blood to the injured part.

The standard military text of the day stated that if a tourniquet had been applied, it should always be removed as soon as possible, to avoid tissue death or gangrene. A tourniquet could be easily overlooked, however, especially under blankets or coats, in the dark, or where hundreds of wounded were crammed together. The tourniquet therefore soon fell into disfavour among medical personnel on Gallipoli, who preferred the direct pressure method, where medics applied finger or fist pressure directly over the artery, wherever possible between the bleeding wound and the heart.

The tourniquet was one of many topics discussed by the Anzac Medical Society. This unique institution was formed on 7 November 1915 in an effort to keep medical officers on Gallipoli up to date on medical, clinical and surgical developments both there and in the rest of the world. It held four meetings at Anzac, and acted as a forum for discussion, exchange of experiences, dissemination of information, and lectures by distinguished visiting consultants. The society was continued on other fronts until 1918.

The equipment used by medical officers in field and hospital units (the latter supplemented by other stores of instruments) came from wood or wicker panniers or cases carried with the unit. The size of these boxes varied with the type of unit. They contained all the instruments necessary for the military physician or surgeon. Generally they sufficed, but some Australian surgeons supplemented their equipment with instruments they either brought with them or purchased from London. All medical units (including the RAPs) were equipped with medical or surgical panniers.

Despite the obvious advantages, and indeed its necessity, X-ray equipment was very rare in the Dardanelles. Fortunately No.1 ASH had its own X-ray machine when it deployed to Mudros, so that from the end of May bullets and shrapnel pieces could be removed there safely. Despite two British stationary hospitals and an Indian hospital being set up at Mudros at the same time, none of those units possessed an X-ray machine. All their patients needing X-ray assessment therefore had to be sent to the Australian hospital.

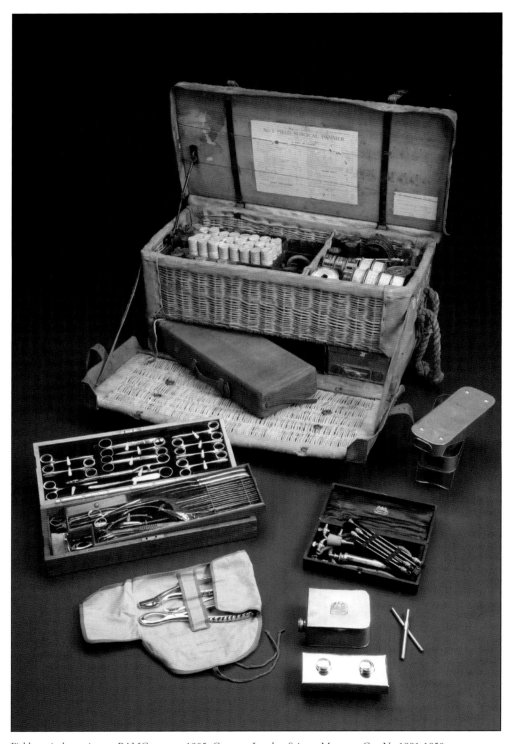

Field surgical pannier set, RAMC pattern, 1905. Courtesy London Science Museum, Cat. No.1981-1850.

ACCOMMODATION, ROUTINE AND SUPPLIES

Facilities at the front were relatively crude throughout the Gallipoli campaign. The 2nd LH Fd Amb accommodated its patients in three large dugouts cut into the side of a hill. These were roofed with tarpaulins, and were each capable of holding 20 to 25 men. A square excavation was also made in which a barely waterproof operating tent was set up.

There was also a sandbag hut that could accommodate 15 patients, but it was not used except for emergencies, as the walls were not secure in wet weather, and the roof could not be made waterproof. Neither timber nor corrugated iron sheeting for the purpose was available at that time on Gallipoli. A large dugout was used as a dispensary, another served as a waiting-room for patients, and could provide additional accommodation in an emergency.

Different units used a variety of schemes to ensure maximum efficiency and conserve manpower. The system used the 2nd LH Fd Amb on Gallipoli can be used for illustration. The unit had four medical officers who operated by night, and carried out routine duties by day. Three of these officers rotated duty as orderly officer for 24 hours, during which time they saw and attended to every case admitted. If an anaesthetist was required, or the number of admissions called for assistance, the orderly officer called the officer next on duty. If even further help was needed, he could call the commander of the field ambulance. The officer who had gone off duty the day before was not likely to be called except in an unusual emergency, and could be sure of a good night's sleep. This also meant that the commanding officer was present whenever anything serious occurred.

The dressing station of the 4th Australian Field Ambulance nestled in the shelter of the appropriately named Rest Gully on Gallipoli. (AWM C00665)

Contents of a pair of a Field Medical Panniers

[1898 Pattern, Weight: approx 41.3 kgs.]

MEDICINES

Acid, Boric – ounces 2

Acid, Carbolic (crystals) in 2 oz. bottles – ounces 8

Acid, Gallic, 5 gr. Tablets - doz. 9

Ammon: Carb., 3 gr. tablets - doz. 16

Antipyrin, 5 gr. Tablets - doz. 10

Argent: Nitrate – ounces 1

Brandy, in 2 oz. bottles - ounces 16

Chloral Hydras: 5 gr. Tablets – doz. 16

Chloroform: in 2 oz. bottles – ounces 16

Ext: Opii Liq – ounces 4

Hydrag: Perchlor: soloids - doz. 12

Ipecac: Pulv: sine Emetine, 5 gr. tablets in 2 oz. bottles – doz. 34

Iodoform: in vulcanite dredger with screw cap – ounces 3

Mistura pro Diarrhoea – ounces 4

Oleum Ment: Pip: - ounces 1

Oleum Olivae – ounces 8

Oleum Ricini, in 2 bottles 16

Oleum Terebinth: - ounces 4

Pil: Blaud: 4 gr. – ounces 4

Pill and tablet tin [containing a variety of tablets] 1

Potass: Bicarb:, 10 gr. tablets – doz. 8.5

Potass: Bromid: 5 gr. tablets - doz. 8

Potass: Permanganus:, 2 gr. tablets - doz. 16

Pulv.: Ipecac: Co: 5 gr. tablets – doz. 21

Quininae Acid: Suplh: 2 gr. tablets in 4 bottles – doz. 92

Quininae Acid: Suplh: 5 gr. tablets in 4 bottles – doz. 33

Sodii Bicarb: 10 gr. tablets – doz. 9

Sodii Salicylas: 5 gr. tablets - doz. 19

Spirit Ammon: Arom: - ounces 8

Tinct: Aconiti: 5 gr. tablets – doz. 17

Tinct: Chlorof: et Morphinae – ounces 3

Tinct: Opii – ounces 4

Zinci Suplh: 5 gr. tablets – doz. 8

INSTRUMENTS ETC

Scissors – pair 1

Spare bottle 1

Specification Tallies and pencil book 1

Spoons, tea 2

Stethoscope, aluminium 1

Tongue depressor 1

[Hypodermic syringes, needles and tablets for same]

[Ophthalmic tablets, various]

[Measures, test tubes, rubber tubing, sprit lamp]

[Bandages, catgut, scissors, thread, needles]

Instruments, tooth, small pouch 1

Tape, pieces of – No: 12

Tourniquet, screw 6

Wool, boric, in 2 oz. Packets 6

Bandages, triangular 12

Bovril, invalid (in 4 oz. tins) lb 1

Knife, for opening tins 1

Meat, extract of (in 4 oz. tins) 1

Warmers, food (spirit lamp) 1

Wool, double cyanide (in 4 oz. packets) 1

[Adhesive plaster, gauze, basins]

Despite the day-to-day workload of the medical units, routine activities such as stretcher drills, health and hygiene inspections, laundry, Q-store, personnel administration, pay, completion of army forms, and ongoing training of AAMC personnel continued. As many of the medical staff at this time would have been reinforcements, and therefore inexperienced, such training was very valuable.

Working conditions were almost as primitive at the Australian hospitals established on Lemnos. By July the dust and fly pest there had become so bad that infection rates soared, forcing the cancellation of many surgical procedures. Almost every hospital unit deployed there initially found that its equipment was either on another ship or 'lost'.

What little equipment No. 3 AGH had in Mudros was obtained from the Red Cross store ship. This unit had over 800 patients to care for, and several of its medical staff including its surgeon, were sick. The only food available was the standard army ration of bully beef and biscuits. All patients were nursed on mattresses on the ground – with adverse effects on staff, who had to lift patients, as well as having to kneel to nurse them. There was no clean clothing, nor were there sufficient eating utensils. Spoons, cups, knives and forks were all loaned from the personal kit of the medical staff.

ONGOING MEDICAL TREATMENT

Once a soldier received first aid he was sent, carried, or made his own way to an RAP, battalion dressing station, or field ambulance. Once there he was classified according to the nature of his wound or complaint. A medical officer advised an NCO where the man was to be sent, and this was recorded on various forms. A ticket or label was made out giving the casualty's name and regimental number, the nature of his complaint, the amount of morphine if given, and finally his destination.

Looking down on Watson's Pier with shells bursting near ANZAC headquarters. No. 1 Australian Casualty Clearing Station is situated on the extreme left of this photograph. (AWM PS1494)

Where large numbers of casualties were involved in April and August, this system broke down. During these periods lightly wounded men could be sent to hospital ships, where space was at a premium, while critically injured men often ended up on an improvised transport or other vessel designated to carry only lightly wounded cases.

The basic function of the aid posts and field ambulances was to facilitate the early evacuation of all serious casualties, subject always to the availability of ships and good weather. In some instances ships, if available, were delayed for reasons other than storms, for example the presence of enemy submarines. Patients were given food and provided with shelter where possible. Morphine was given for pain, wounds dressed where necessary, and fractures splinted. Wounds were not closed except on Lemnos or in Cairo where, with the assistance of X-rays, it could be established that no foreign bodies had been left *in situ*.

When a medical unit became big enough to deal with a relatively large number of cases, it had to streamline its limited facilities in the best way possible. The *RAMC Training Manual* set out guidelines for sorting casualties and organising the activities of medical units. These activities included receiving, recording, and classifying wounded (on both their arrival and discharge); looking after severe and light cases; and the dying. Places were also selected and marked out for cooking, the reception of arms and accoutrements, latrines, and a mortuary.

However, not every unit had the luxury of such organisation. The dressing station operated by Captain P.A. Davenport (5th Fd Amb) consisted of two wooden boxes for patients to sit on, with no overhead cover; it was completely exposed to rifle fire. 'Dressings were very scarce most of the wounds having to be dressed with the first field dressing'. There were no splints of any kind, and very little morphine for relieving pain. 'Many of the men with dysentery had not the strength to reach the latrines, and consequently the ground all round was polluted.'

WOUNDS AND TREATMENT

Field ambulances were not supposed to attempt operations at Anzac. Casualties with abdominal wounds were rested, given nothing by mouth, and moved only if necessary. Because the only chance of survival for this category of patient lay in speedy evacuation, their prognosis was almost always bad. Where a soldier was suffering severe pain he could be given opium. Chest wounds, particularly where bleeding into the lungs (haemothorax) was involved, were another wound category not treated on the peninsula.

On Gallipoli one of the golden rules was never to remove foreign bodies such as bullets or shrapnel from wounds, thereby opening the wound again before medical evacuation offshore. Instead, such casualties were evacuated to a base hospital with the object *in situ*. The peculiar circumstances of Gallipoli often worked against such a practice, however, particularly during bad weather, and many bullets were removed surgically at Anzac, and this operation was certainly performed on hospital ships.

Conditions prevailing on Gallipoli were not conducive to rapid healing, and even the smallest cuts and abrasions were likely to become infected. The medical condition was known as Barcoo Rot, or Veldt Sore from the Boer War (South Africa 1899-1902). Dressings applied to these types of wounds were 'wet' (packed with gauze saturated in an antiseptic solution).

With larger wounds, the doctor was required to clean the wound site thoroughly. Removing dead tissue was considered very important. As soldiers with large wounds were often in great pain when dressings were applied or changed, hydrogen peroxide was applied with a spray bottle. The application of a strip of gauze or lint spread with soft Vaseline ointment was used to remove dressings from amputation stumps.

Water – both for drinking and for preparing antiseptics – was always scarce. This was the case in the Australian sector on Gallipoli particularly, and on Lemnos generally. Sudden severe storms, which often blew down large parts of the tented hospitals there, were yet another trial for Australian units looking after wounded on Lemnos. Wood for building, for reinforcing dugouts and trenches, and for cooking fires was also scarce.

Some experienced surgeons who joined the AIF were appalled at the eagerness with which their juniors operated, particularly on board hospital ships. By the end of the campaign, operations were performed only rarely while a casualty was in transit from the front to a base hospital. Due to the early enthusiasm of some surgeons, some casualties died who might otherwise have stood a chance of survival – this was particularly the case with abdominal wounds. Many articles in medical journals of the time stress that early surgical intervention was often fatal with abdominal wounds.

Shock had long been recognised as a potential killer, and it was treated on Gallipoli in the same manner prescribed by any first aid manual of that time – warmth, blankets, and occasionally medicinal brandy. In treating shock the most widely used drug was morphine, often combined with atropine when used for this purpose. The atropine helped prevent the vomiting that sometimes ensued when only morphine was given. For casualties with serious head, chest or abdominal injuries, vomiting often had fatal consequences.

Saline transfusions were not unknown, and these were also given where bleeding had been severe, to raise blood pressure by introducing more fluid into the circulation. Blood transfusions were not carried out at this period of the war.

Unlike on the Western Front in France and Belgium, where troops were fighting in soil that had been manured for generations, the incidence of tetanus on Gallipoli was very low. Still, tetanus antitoxin was used throughout the campaign as a first aid measure for very contaminated wounds, and from July it was given for all types of wounds in a prophylactic dose. Australian troops were also inoculated against the traditional scourge of armies, which had decimated previous military forces – cholera. Across the trenches typhus (against which the AIF had been inoculated) made huge inroads into the Ottoman army. Areas of the peninsula were also malaria prone.

The famous blizzard of November 1915 has been well documented elsewhere. It should be stated that the British in this instance fared worse than the Australians or New Zealanders, due mainly to their greater exposure, deeper trenches, and inadequate winter clothing. The Australian medical services did have their share of frostbite to contend with, but on a much smaller scale than was suffered at either Suvla Bay or Cape Helles.

Australian and New Zealand positions were more sheltered, and sentries and front-line troops had received an issue of waterproof clothing. Even so, many Diggers suffered from exposure. Alcohol was the standard remedy. One medical officer of the 5th Fd Amb dispensed 14 bottles of brandy, 18 bottles of port wine and 46 bottles of stout over a 56-day period.

To make matters worse, water pipes burst in the cold, and for a time water was restricted to less than two litres per day. Some doctors recorded that it was very difficult to operate on patients under canvas, owing to the heavy frosts.

SURGERY

Then, as now, the decision to operate was a difficult one. If a soldier could endure evacuation by sea, he stood a better chance from an operation either on board a fully fitted-out hospital ship or in a base hospital. Sometimes, however, where the case was critical and the medical officer knew that transport was not available, he had no choice but to intervene. The lack of facilities and the greater chance of infection made the undertaking a difficult one. An Australian surgeon noted in his diary that the contents of soldiers' pockets were often found in the abdominal cavity; occasionally there were cartridge clips, and once, the cap of a shell.

Operations performed on the peninsula by Australian units were invariably performed in or under tents, although the clearing station could, by late October, boast the luxury of a concrete floor and linen sheets on the walls of its operating theatre. The facilities of the 2nd LH Fd Amb were somewhat primitive, and of course asepsis (a surgical technique that makes the entire space in which an operation is to be performed sterile) was impossible under such conditions. The operating table was improvised by simply placing a stretcher on two large panniers.

At the 4th Fd Amb, pieces of four-by-four timber sunk into the ground supported a stretcher at a convenient height – again, the stretcher served as the operating table. At its head was the anaesthetist's table, while in one corner were basins, water and disinfectants for sterilising the hands of the medical team. In another corner were a mechanical steriliser and the means for cleaning the patient's skin and wounds. Towels and dressing were also kept in the tent.

For lighting, two acetylene-fuelled operating theatre lamps, suspended from the roof, were used. Most units used a Dietz hurricane lamp as an emergency light source. One was always kept fuelled and ready to be put in use the moment the other went out. A small acetylene-fuelled bicycle lamp was used for abdominal work, as this was more portable, and could be held relatively close to the wound. A Sawyers Stove outside was used to boil water. Towels and swabs were sterilised by keeping them in a solution of 1:40 carbolic acid, and simply wringing them out when required.

Dugouts of the 2nd and 3rd Australian Field Ambulances at Anzac Cove. Note the telephone lines. Allied dugouts were not as well constructed or equipped as those of the enemy. (AWM C01734)

Lack of foresight was sometimes evident in treating casualties. An example is the *Gloucester Castle* in August. While it possessed an X-ray machine, there was no radiographer aboard, nor were there any hydrogen peroxide or drainage tubes. The ship carried only eight or ten scalpels for operating, a few pairs of pressure forceps, no skull forceps, insufficient carbolic acid, hardly any catgut for ligaturing blood vessels, and no eye instruments at all. At this time, the ship had more than 500 badly wounded men aboard.

The most frequently used anaesthetic was chloroform. However, open ether was the preferred anaesthetic in amputations, as patients suffering from septic infections were considered to be at greater risk with chloroform. Very few amputations were performed on Gallipoli, unless the limbs were hopelessly shattered.

HEAD INJURIES

Soldiers who sustained head injuries sometimes had a better chance of recovery than those with abdominal and chest wounds. Again, operations in the field were undertaken only when imperative. Soldiers who were engaged in lookout or spotting duties in the trenches received a number of facial and head injuries. These injuries, and the loss of eyes, were often the result of the mirror at the top of trench periscopes being smashed by an enemy bullet, and fragments entering the eye.

The AIF was fortunate to have some of Australia's leading eye specialists working as officers in the AAMC. One of these was Major John Lockhart Gibson, who worked from a few tents at Mudros, having brought with him much of his own personal equipment. He arranged for all eye cases not hopelessly injured to come to No. 3 AGH from both Gallipoli and other medical units on Lemnos.

Lack of transport often prevented troops with injured eyes from being landed at Lemnos, however, and they were shipped directly to Alexandria. The four day journey was sufficient in many cases to ensure the permanent loss of eyes that otherwise could have been saved by Gibson's unit at Mudros, where he had ophthalmological instruments not available even in some of the large hospitals in Cairo and Malta.

Other surgeons were critical of the primitive conditions on Gallipoli. Captain J.R. Muirhead related how in May, after one trip, he returned to Anzac on the *Arcadian*, which picked up 500 wounded men. Wards had not been arranged on board, and there was so little equipment that he had to remove hopelessly damaged eyes with a pair of old scissors.

Foreign bodies in the eye were never probed under field conditions. One of the surgeons at No. 1 AGH in Cairo noted the frequency of penetrating wounds of the eye from the glass of the trench periscope. He was exasperated by having to remove an eye, and find the foreign bodies that caused its destruction were eyelashes carried in by a fragment of glass that had been removed unsatisfactorily at the time.

Where the eardrum had been perforated due to an injury, treatment was simply a matter of preventing further injury or infection until the soldier reached advanced medical care. Syringing, or the use of eardrops or hydrogen peroxide, were considered dangerous.

FRACTURES

The initial treatment for most fractures was to immobilise them by using rigid splints. It became the practice on Gallipoli for soldiers suffering compound fractures of their lower limbs to have the foot of the injured leg tied to the handle of the stretcher and then be carried head first down a gully, providing automatic traction to the injured limb. Where custom-made splints were in short supply, they were improvised from sticks or a rifle. Application of the latter was written into military lore with the caution: 'Remove the bolt and see that the rifle or magazine contains no cartridges'.

Surgeons were faced with the dilemma whether or not to open up the wound around the broken bone to examine the extent of the fracture and the associated damage. This was particularly relevant where a fracture had been caused by a gunshot wound. Not a great deal could be done for spinal injuries, many of whom died from complications, and the movement necessitated by the many stages in the evacuation chain.

Soldier using a periscope rifle. A homemade invention of mirrors, boxwood and wire, the periscope rifle allowed the user to sight and fire a rifle over the parapet without exposing himself to enemy fire. (AWM A05767)

TREATMENT ON HOSPITAL SHIPS

Conditions for the treatment of casualties were better on hospital ships, although as we have seen there were exceptions, especially in late April. Wounded placed aboard transport ships hastily nominated as ambulance carriers, or 'black ships', (as they were not painted in the internationally recognised colour of white) fared less well.

Even in these relative havens of safety there were problems. Surgeons found it difficult to get satisfactory X-ray photographs of the skull, owing to the vibration and movement of the ship, while nursing patients was also awkward, due to the arrangement of cots and beds, which had very little space between them. This also meant that it was almost impossible to apply adequate extension to fractured limbs. Simply getting on board a ship also did not always mean a casualty's problems were over, as army stretchers would not fit into ships' lifts. There had been no inter-Service drills beforehand that might have identified this as a problem.

During the April landing such surgical resources as there were aboard the ships were strained to the limit. On one such ship, immediately after the landing, there had been little time for adequate preparation. The mess tables and benches previously used by the troops were still in position, together with all the litter, debris and filth produced by the hundreds of troops who had just disembarked.

Operating facilities were basic. A mess table was set apart for operations in one corner of a cabin. There was a primus stove for sterilising instruments, and cotton wool was used for swabs. On the operating table itself, wounded soldiers were anaesthetised by a medic, often still in dirty and blood-stained clothes (the operation area alone was uncovered, and surrounded by wet boiled towels).

The AAMC rendered effective treatment in the field for the duration of the campaign. Standards of treatment suffered during periods in which medical resources were over-strained, as in late April and early August. The other major external influences on how casualties were managed were the number of medical personnel available, the supply of medicines and equipment, the speed with which casualties could be cleared from Gallipoli, and the weather. The last two factors, particularly medical evacuation, were largely beyond the control of the AAMC.

CHAPTER 5:

Casualty Evacuation

As AAMC units or their personnel were engaged further away from Gallipoli, they coped less well. This situation applied along the chain of evacuation, on hospital ships and transports, until the Australian base hospitals in Egypt were reached. These were again under the more immediate supervision of Australians, rather than Imperial officers. The AAMC therefore worked best when it controlled its own spheres of activity directly.

Medical arrangements were in a continual state of flux and readjustment, and were particularly strained in April and August 1915. A gradual improvement in some aspects of medical evaluation was offset by the increase of disease and sickness in the AIF. Lessons were learned, however, and solutions worked out wherever possible.

To appreciate the difficulties involved in arranging in arranging for the transport of wounded and sick troops, an understanding of Lines of Communication is critical. In July 1915 (taken here as a representative of the entire campaign), these consisted of:

1. the port of Alexandria in Egypt, two to three days' voyage from Mudros, depending on the weather.

2. the immediate base at Mudros on the island of Lemnos.

3. the advanced base at Imbros, where GHQ was situated; and

4. the landing beaches on Gallipoli, which had both naval and military medical, supply, and transport staffs.

Interdependence on the Lines of Communisation was such that congestion at one point had serious consequences for the next link in the chain. As AAMC units were obliged to work within the constraints of this system, they were largely helpless as regards much of the offshore medical transportation.

Several factors lay behind the breakdown in the medical evacuation of casualties from Anzac. First, there was the complexity of a combined amphibious operation, requiring communication facilities that would not become available until more recent times. Second, there was a failure by senior British army staff to consult with medical staff officers, to allow them to plan ahead, based on an incorrect assumption that hospital and staff reinforcements would be required only on a temporary basis.

The third factor was the sheer impossibility of triaging wounded on the beaches before they were evacuated during late April and early August. Finally, there was the poor liaison and communication between the different branches of the MEF, and between senior officers within the various medical services, British and Australian.

The system of evacuation of wounded from Gallipoli varied as attempts were made to adapt to changes in the tactical situation and to create the most efficient system. The diagram illustrates the general evacuation process from Anzac. As can be seen there are several features, particularly distance, which set it apart from the evacuation process as it operated on the Western Front in France and Belgium.

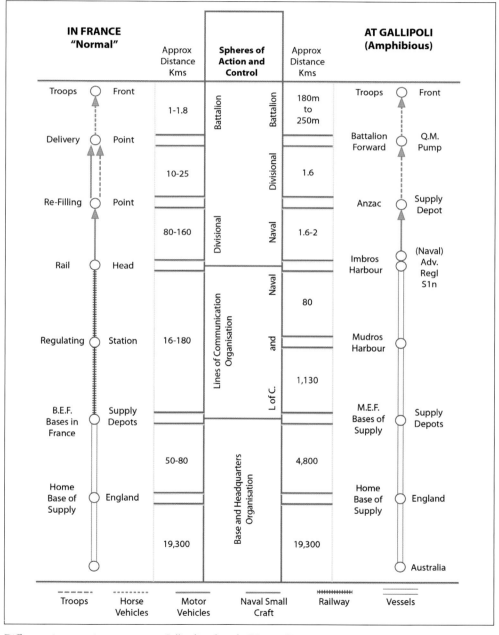

Differences in evacuation processes on Gallipoli and on the Western Front.

AT THE FRONT

Many troops were shot even before they leapt from their boats at Anzac Cove on 25 April. By early morning, a constant and opposing stream of wounded trying to reach the safety of the ships met men trying to disembark. To compound the chaos there was a shortage of small boats. While munitions and men were being landed on the narrow beach, what little space was available rapidly filled with the dead, wounded and dying. Only after April, when the MEF began to consolidate its precarious foothold on the peninsula, did an effective system of evacuation start to evolve.

The only formed medical unit to go ashore on 25 April was No. 1 ACCS. The tent subdivisions of the field ambulances that were part of the force, and which had been placed on the troopships, had to remain on board to deal with wounded being sent from the beach. Apart from small groups of doctors and other AAMC personnel organic to infantry units, only the bearer subdivisions of the ambulances landed. Lack of headway meant that all heavy equipment, tents and wheeled transport (which were never used) were left on board the troopships. Later, the tent subdivisions were brought ashore and set up dressing posts to treat minor wounds and sickness.

An unidentified AAMC bearer, his Red Cross brassard just visible on his right sleeve, stands next to a wounded soldier who is lying on an improvised stretcher carriage pulled by two donkeys. These donkeys, usually 'on loan' from Indian Army units on Gallipoli, were often borrowed by medics and AAMC and infantry stretcher-bearers. (AWM A01522)

The first link in the evacuation chain was often provided by the casualty's mate. This mutual care was, and continues to be, a feature of warfare. Sergeant C.F. Laseron of the 13th Battalion related his experiences as a casualty, which, while not typical of all casualties (he was deliberately shot at by the Turks while assisting a wounded man), provides an extreme example of the progress of a casualty from receiving a wound to being evacuated.

While attending his wounded mate, Laseron was shot in the foot. The impact threw him down the hillside into a trench, where he was impaled by two bayonets fixed to rifles lying against the side of the parapet. His comrades lifted him off and he fainted. After he regained consciousness he spent three hours crawling more than a kilometre (all the way subject to sniper fire) to a dressing station. There his wound was dressed and he was placed on a donkey for the trip to the beach.

More usually though, wounded were removed from the field by their own regimental stretcher-bearers. Retrieving casualties was far from routine, and there were many feats of heroism and endurance. Wounded were first taken to the RAP for elementary first aid by the RMO, who was assisted by an AAMC NCO and one other medic.

From the RAP, stretcher-bearers from the field ambulances came forward to the trenches and to take casualties to dressing posts. These bearers were usually sourced from the tent subdivisions of field ambulances. From there another relay of bearers carried them to the main dressing station run by the ambulance.

Casualties were triaged, then either evacuated or kept for up to three days in one of the tented wards of the field ambulance. If evacuation was necessary, patients were removed to the CCS, where they were stabilised and any urgent surgical procedures carried out before they were placed on barges for the trip out to the hospital ships, if these were available.

Although only relatively short distances were involved in evacuating soldiers overland on Gallipoli, the ruggedness of the terrain and the steep slopes often made the journey a hazardous one. An illustration is the path taken by bearers from Quinn's Post to the beach, a distance of about three kilometres.

The route was along narrow tracks that became hazardous when wet. These tracks were usually crowded with men and pack animals carrying stores and ammunition, rubbish, water cans, and rations. Often, they were favourite target areas for Ottoman snipers. In winter, bearers slipped or fell into water filled holes. Another hazard was signallers' wire, which could be found at various heights and on the ground, at times tripping or nearly hanging the unwary. The diagram on page 74 illustrates how this system worked.

At other places the trenches were so narrow that the wounded could only be transported through them on the few short naval stretchers then available, or by draping them in a blanket or waterproof sheet and dragging them along. Some medical officers, no doubt advised by their men, improvised sleds or special slides to reduce casualty rates among their own bearers, and to spare the wounded as much pain as possible. Two rifles passed through the sleeves of a buttoned overcoat made a popular substitute for stretchers.

Eventually improvements, in the form of wider tracks and sandbag barricades built at exposed points, made life a little easier for bearers and their patients. Increasingly engineer units and the navy were able to make and provide limited numbers of stretchers, lessening the acute shortage.

The evacuations during the August Offensive, although better organised offshore, were little better on land then they had been in April, due to the unexpectedly high number of casualties, which again swamped the system. In addition, by August the strength of unit and field ambulance medical personnel was seriously depleted by sickness.

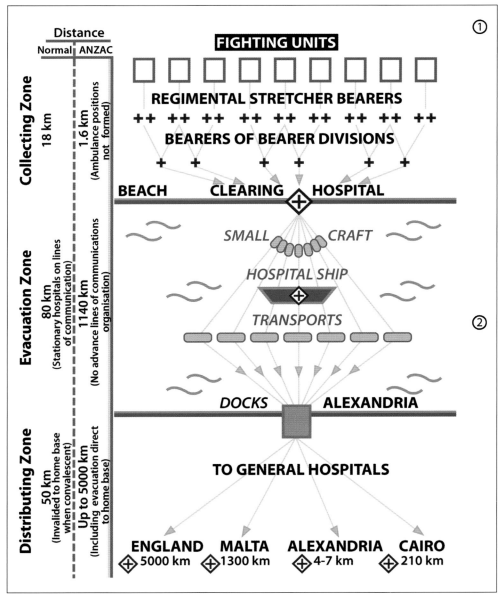

Scheme of medical evacuation from Anzac.

AAMC units on Gallipoli received few reinforcements. Despite the rigours of the campaign, most medical personnel struggled on until they also succumbed to dysentery or other diseases. What medical reinforcements did arrive from Australia and New Zealand were diverted in Egypt to staff crowded hospitals in Cairo. The AAMC on Lemnos was similarly affected, despite a total of 590 Australian doctors, nurses and ORs arriving as reinforcements in Egypt in June and July.

Matters were made worse for their New Zealand Army Medical Corps (NZAMC) colleagues when all medical students serving in New Zealand field ambulances were recalled to their universities at the end of July. Australia did not follow suit until after the December evacuation, when all fourth year medical students were returned to Australia to complete their studies.

As the fighting dragged on, staff shortages worsened. By October, despite the arrival of the 2nd Division from late August, the shortfall in AAMC personnel was 24 medical officers and 357 ORs. The HQ staff of the 1st Division believed its medical services would collapse in the face of any serious attack or offensive, and advised GHQ to that effect. At that time the only medical reinforcements scheduled for the 1st Division for October and November were 42 AAMC ORs, but no medical officers.

SHORE TO SHIP

Ships used in the Gallipoli campaign for transporting wounded were classified as:

HOSPITAL SHIPS, which were either purpose-built, or more usually (and in Australia's case), requisitioned liners extensively adapted for the particular purpose of accommodating the sick and wounded. They were floating hospitals, and were medically and surgically equipped to deal with all cases of injury and disease; they were painted white overall, with a horizontal band of green, about a metre and a half wide, around the hull. At night the hulls were brilliantly illuminated, and there were usually long rows of red and green lights along their sides. They were protected under international law from attack.

HOSPITAL CARRIERS were inferior types of hospital ships, generally being passenger liners or merchant vessels that had been fitted out as well as time permitted. They carried the distinctive markings of hospital ships, and were also registered under the Geneva Convention.

AMBULANCE TRANSPORTS, or 'black ships', while equipped to carry and tend the sick and wounded, were also used on return journeys to transport troops and stores. These vessels did not carry the distinguishing marks of hospital ships, and could not claim protection. At Anzac these ships therefore could not take on wounded within the firing zone, close to shore. They were sometimes in a dirty state, particularly if they had carried horses and mules.

Hospital ships were actually the province of the army, not the navy, a fact that the military seemed slow to realise. To further complicate matters, hospital ships received their sailing orders from the senior naval medical officer, and details of their destination from an army medical officer.

The unprecedented degree of naval and military cooperation called for by the Gallipoli operation meant that the responsibility for evacuating casualties became divided. Australian medical units were involved both at the beach and on the various transport ships and ferries, and to a lesser extent on sea transport.

Maritime assets such as ships (but not hospital ships, the province of the army) came under the navy, which provided Beach Masters (traffic controllers) to manage small boat traffic. On the Anzac sector's beach, small boats were loaded under the direction of an officer of No. 1 ACCS, while boats' crews, under the command of the Beach Master, off-loaded them at the other end.

Wounded being embarked on a hospital ship via box stretcher and hoist. Such procedures were impossible in bad weather or rough seas. (AWM P01531.007)

Executive responsibility for the stage of evacuation between the piers and a ship's deck was strictly naval. However, once at the ship's rail, army units took over the remaining stages, including sea transport to base hospitals in Egypt and elsewhere. The shore to ship link was the most trouble-prone step in the overall process of removing wounded from Gallipoli. Its complexity, and the ways it evolved are illustrated in the diagram below.

Efficient medical evacuation was plagued by an inability on the part of Hamilton's general staff to plan for realistic casualty figures. An illustration is provided by the initial allocation in early April of six launches, each capable of holding twelve cots – for 75,000 troops.

By the afternoon of 25 April, Major J. Gordon of No. 1 ACCS was the last of his unit left aboard the *Ionian*. He and 15 of his own men, five of whom were sick, looked on from the deck at the slaughter on the beach. As with all the other troopships, no preparation had been made on board in case casualties occurred or the landing failed.

Shortly after, several barges carrying 450 wounded men came alongside. As the *Ionian* had no means of getting them aboard, it had to launch its own boats to transfer the casualties. It is possible that Gordon's commanding officer ashore, Giblin, was aware that if nothing else, at least the *Ionian* had medical staff aboard, and could assist. He may have despatched those wounded to that ship. It was a desperate, if understandable, move on his part. Reinforcements in the form of the 2nd Division, with its medical units, would not arrive for another four months.

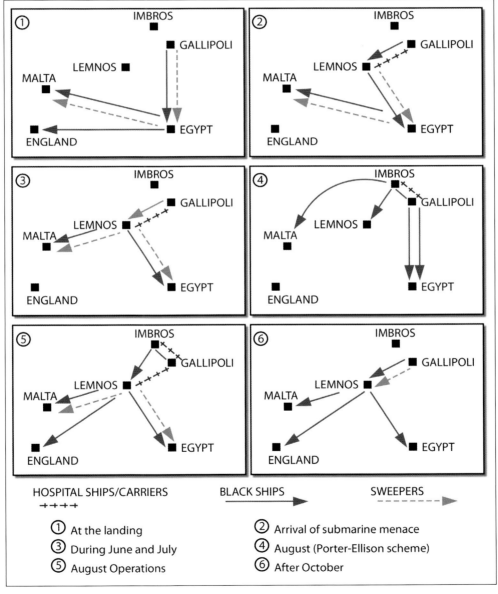

The evolution in maritime evacuation.

Small boats and barges were very scarce during the landing itself, and for weeks after, and some extraordinary efforts were made to obtain anything that could float to evacuate the wounded. As one example, a group of volunteers managed to refloat a large lighter that had run aground loaded with kerosene tins full of fresh water. With it and two other boats left abandoned alongside a pontoon, they were able to evacuate about 150 stretcher cases and a similar number of walking wounded.

The military situation demanded that the disembarkation of the fighting troops, their ammunition and rations should have first priority, and all available craft were directed to this objective. In these difficult circumstances, Hamilton adhered to the principle that tactical requirements must take priority.

In quieter periods, for example from mid-May to early August, the evacuation of wounded was a relatively ordered procedure. A hospital ship lowered a long wooden box over the side, the stretcher case was placed in it, and it was raised to the deck where he was received by waiting orderlies and whisked away to a ward for diagnosis and washing. Some ships used a steam hoist to effect the rapid loading of patients.

Then there was the sea. Private L.E. Schaffer, an AAMC orderly who served for a time on the *Karoola*, wrote of the inconveniences of a rough sea, which was so bad that by midnight he was 'sprinting in great style as fifty percent of the patients were seasick in addition to their other complaints'.

While more personnel were available in July and August, and the organisation of the hospital ships had certainly improved, there were still not sufficient ships or personnel in the Mediterranean to meet the demand. There was always an imbalance between the demand and what resources were procurable. Later evidence points to the severe shortage of suitable ships, the lead-time to refit them, and the fact that the allies were fighting not only on Gallipoli - a sideshow - but in an increasingly voracious war in France and an evolving campaign in Egypt and Palestine. The demand for shipping was enormous.

There were also concerns about inadequate hospital accommodation. In Cairo Maxwell, who ultimately controlled the hospital ships, advised Hamilton on 8 May that he had arranged almost 12,000 hospital beds in Egypt. He also suggested that for the 'short' 48-hour journey from the Dardanelles to Alexandria, it was not necessary to have dedicated hospital ships, as these were badly needed for the longer voyage to Britain.

Lance-Corporal J.G. Burgess of the 6th Light Horse Regiment, who was suffering from dysentery, wrote of his experiences in July of being evacuated to a hospital ship, and how he was then cared for. After waiting in a field ambulance shelter until a boat was ready to take the day's sick and wounded out to the ship, he was embarked on the *Rewa* and given something to eat. He was then examined and moved into a ward. But this was during a quiet time in the campaign.

In August, due mainly to the lack of hospital ships, it was proposed to make Imbros the clearing centre for evacuation by transports carrying casualties from Gallipoli. From there temporary hospital ships would take them to Mudros, Alexandria or Malta. Although self-propelled beetles (shallow, steel-hulled craft with a drawbridge, capable of holding 500 men) were to be used for the Suvla Bay landing, none were set aside for the evacuation of wounded and, as in April, no craft were allocated for the exclusive use of the medical services.

The navy's senior medical officer in the Mediterranean, Porter, arrived on the scene shortly before the August operations began, and was appalled by the inadequacies of the medical evacuation scheme for this second great operation in the campaign. In July Birrell had proposed a scheme for evacuating wounded during the August Offensive. This plan provided for all six available hospital ships to be on station off Anzac and Cape Helles, backed up by a further 30 transport ships.

Hamilton's staff radically reduced Birrell's request for many more medical staff, including the use of 1000 Egyptian stretcher-bearers. Porter also altered Birrell's plan on 28 July, as he believed that there were still too few hospital ships. On 6 August he drew up what came to be known as the Porter-Ellison Scheme.

Under this scheme eight hospital ships, in conjunction with a number of trawlers, would maintain a short ferry service to Imbros, transferring cases there to ambulance carriers. Evacuation to Egypt would be mainly by 'black ships' with some medical staff aboard, and by any other available hospital ships.

On 6 August eight hospital ships were indeed available at the Dardanelles. Of the 25 transports earmarked by the Admiralty as 'black ships', however, only nine had been prepared, while another was serving as a depot ship for medical and nursing personnel. Eleven others failed to materialise, and four of the vessels specified were found to be totally unsuitable. To make matters worse, these vessels were forbidden to transmit messages by wireless.

Lieutenant-General G.F. Ellison was the Deputy Quartermaster-General (DQMG) of the MEF. With his assistance, Porter planned to have every hospital ship lie off Gallipoli in such a way that at least one fully equipped hospital ship would be available at each of the beaches throughout the operations.

The plan called for all wounded to be taken directly to waiting hospital ships, where they would be quickly triaged on deck, serious cases being retained on board, and the lightly wounded passed across to trawlers moored on the opposite side of the ship. These would take the lightly wounded to hospital carriers harboured in Kephalos at Imbros. As 'black ships' were not protected by the Geneva Convention, they could not anchor any closer to the Gallipoli peninsula.

Given the lack of time to prepare adequately, this evacuation scheme had serious deficiencies. Apart from relying on fair weather and an unlimited supply of hospital carriers, the scarcity of small craft in the harbours of both Lemnos and Imbros substantially hindered operations. The Porter-Ellison Scheme foundered on poor communications and the lack of sufficient transport. As it happened, the weather over 7-8 August was poor, with rough seas, which delayed the unloading of wounded from ships as well as impeding the passage of ships from Kephalos.

During the August Offensive, three piers were in use on Gallipoli for the evacuation of Australian and New Zealand wounded. From south to north these were No. 1 pier (at Anzac Cove), No. 2 (opposite Russell's Top), and No. 3 (almost opposite Chailak Dere). No. 3 was understaffed, and could be used only at full tide. No. 2, although a safe pier, was undermanned, leaving No 1. as the only fully functioning pier capable of taking large numbers of casualties (see Map 2.3 on page 40).

As in April, the arrangements on the beach itself were less than satisfactory. One of the Beach Masters at Anzac, Commander C.C. Dix, RN, was wounded, and another officer, Captain V. Vyvyan, RN, who was also on the beach, was appointed to direct operations immediately before the actual offensive began. He assumed the overall naval command on the beach.

Captain J.R. Drummond, RN, then came ashore to fill the gap left by Vyvyan, and landed right in the middle of evacuating wounded, on the details of which process he does not appear to have been fully briefed. Despite Porter's elaborate and meticulous preparations, the medical plan as it affected Anzac beach again began to unravel.

On Lemnos the medical situation actually deteriorated even while the August Offensive was being prepared. As fresh troops and materiel poured into Mudros harbour, what organisation was in place for their control teetered on collapse. Again, there were insufficient small craft for handling stores and men. Three launches had been donated by the Red Cross for the exclusive use of the medical services at Mudros, but did not arrive there until late in November.

Due to the lack of engineering preparation with respect to the construction of piers, all ships had to lie about 500 metres from shore because of their draught. There were still few jetties and almost no port facilities, as GHQ had insisted on returning to Egypt a contractor who was sent specifically to oversee the building of piers.

Convalescing on Lemnos. This is as close to the fighting as Australian nurses came. Their contribution, particularly to troop morale, was significant. (IWM Q13720)

The supply of barges was inadequate during the August Offensive. The increasing numbers of casualties on the beach were exposed to shellfire, or suffered from showers of dropping bullets. Many were killed or wounded again while waiting for evacuation. Alarmed senior medical officers of the 1st Division approached Birdwood, which must have had the desired effect, as by 0400 on 8 August eight hospital ships hove into sight. They sent many small launches and picket boats to the shore.

A few days later Colonel Charles Begg, the acting ADMS of the NZ&A Division, and the senior medical officer in the ANZAC sector, brought the precarious situation to Godley's notice. Godley immediately gave him a large number of infantry to assist the overworked medical teams on the beach. Several barges then appeared, and by the night of 12 August the beach was practically cleared of wounded. There was by then an adequate reserve of hospital ships.

These barges relied on being towed by steam pinnaces that were prone to breakdown and shelling, which holed many. More importantly, they had only a limited capacity for water and fuel, both of which had to be replenished at regular intervals, and at times their absences are clearly explained by this need.

The whole matter of resupply appears not to have received the attention it deserved in planning the offensive. The supply of small craft therefore varied, depending on the time of day, the severity of shelling (which sometimes meant leaving those already on board to take their chance until the shelling eased), and the length of time it took to load and unload casualties.

On 7 August the *Delta* and *Dunluce Castle* collected wounded according to plan, and left Anzac for Imbros. However, instead of releasing their wounded to transport ships at Imbros and returning immediately to their station off Anzac, they were sent to Lemnos. The changed arrangements arose from adverse tidal conditions, poor weather, and the overcrowding of Imbros' inadequate harbour at Kephalos.

From 8 August Porter's plan was so strained that the earlier practice of using sweepers to carry casualties directly from Anzac to Mudros was resumed. At Mudros the only large vessel in the harbour on 13 August was the huge 45,000 ton liner *Aquitania*, which was sent to Britain with only a skeleton nursing staff, but a full load of wounded, as by then neither Egypt nor Malta had any hospital accommodation available.

A less obvious reason for the breakdown is partly recorded in Porter's own log. It was the failure of the military medical authorities at Mudros, quartered aboard the *Aragon*. Porter's orders were in envelopes addressed to each ship. Unknown to him, however, key medical planning staff were stranded on board *Aragon* due to the lack of small craft, and could not distribute his orders. Whereas some of the ships earmarked for Anzac (*Delta*, *Sicilia*, *Dunluce Castle* and *Seang Choon*) did receive their own orders directly from Porter, others did not. This was remedied as rapidly as possible by oral explanation and rough notes of the general scheme, given by Porter's staff to the ships in question.

The severity of the fighting in those furious days in early August is reflected by the casualty figures. At the beginning of the action there were three hospital ships off Anzac Cove – *Gascon*, *Devanha*, and *Dongola*. By the first evening all were full. It was the same off the beaches at Cape Helles in the south and Suvla Bay in the north.

Under Porter's scheme these three ships should have proceeded immediately to Mudros, but his orders had not been relayed to the captains of the hospital ships. This explains why they remained off Anzac Cove, even though they were crammed with wounded. The reserve hospital ships did not come on station, as their officers assumed that the three ships at Anzac still had spare capacity. Other mistakes were less forgivable.

An Australian nurse, Sister Ilma Lovell, was seconded to the French transport *Formosa*, which sailed to Suvla Bay for the offensive. Those aboard wondered why no wounded were sent out after their arrival. As she was still flying the French flag, not a Red Cross flag, evacuation officers on shore ignored *Formosa*. Eventually someone realised that something was amiss, and as soon as the Red Cross flag was hoisted, masses of wounded men were rushed aboard, 16 hours after the ship's arrival. Many wounds had become flyblown and septic during the delay, and numerous amputations had to be performed that could have been avoided by earlier evacuation.

Hospital Ship Gascon. (Jeff Isaacs)

HOSPITAL SHIPS, HOSPITAL CARRIERS AND BLACK SHIPS

As black ships showed no lights during the night, they were indistinguishable from other vessels. This added to the distress of medical personnel on naval tows trying to find somewhere to deliver their wounded, who were also usually wet, hungry and seasick. Due to shelling during the day, most black ships had to move further out to sea, away from their pre-arranged locations, making it difficult, if not impossible, for small boat crews to locate them.

After the April landing, in spite of the acute shortage of doctors, Birrell refused the navy's offer to place its medical resources at the army's disposal. Birrell rejected this help because naval surgeons were obliged to return to their ships each night, as the fleet was on active duty and could be deployed anywhere at short notice.

Vice-Admiral Rosslyn Wemyss, who made the suggestion, later recalled that he was shocked when the offer was refused. He then went personally to see Hamilton to protest. This had the desired effect, and 14 naval surgeons were distributed among those black ships without a medical officer. Wemyss had to intervene again in August.

The names of ships such as the *Galeka*, *Saturnia* and *Lutzow* (see page 36) remain as infamous reminders of the deficiencies, in some cases preventable, in the care of wounded from Gallipoli. The *Galeka* illustrates the bungled arrangements for the evacuation of wounded troops by sea. Elements of the AAMC were on board, as part of an amalgam of medical personnel sent to deal with what was often an unknown quantity of wounded.

According to the senior medical officer on board *Galeka*, Lieutenant-Colonel Roderick Tate-Sutherland of the 1st LH Fd Amb, owing to a misunderstanding food and medical equipment belonging to his unit were left in a barge going ashore, and this contributed to the situation. Muirhead, Tate-Sutherland's second-in-command, had been on *Galeka* for three days, during which 'wounded patients had to remain in soiled linen; no clean shirts were obtainable to replace blood stained ones'.

In spite of an attempt to stop him boarding a supply ship in Mudros Bay, *Galeka*'s captain obtained a supply of 300 shirts, but other medical comforts were virtually non-existent on *Galeka*. The ship was ordered to return with only four doctors and 25 orderlies, although it carried over 400 seriously wounded patients. Ironically, while *Galeka* was at Mudros several days earlier, the New Zealand Mounted Fd Amb, consisting of four medical officers and 73 ORs, was ordered to disembark.

Then, just as some semblance of order was being established on Gallipoli, a new menace appeared – the submarine. The fleet received information from Gibraltar on 7 May that a number of German submarines had passed the Straits.

On 13 May, in full view of troops dug in along the peninsula, the battleship HMS *Goliath* sank in two minutes after being torpedoed, with the loss of 520 men. On 25 May the German submarine *U51* sank HMS *Triumph* (off Anzac) and HMS *Majestic* (off Cape Helles). The *U51* also attempted to torpedo HMS *Vengeance*, HMS *Lord Nelson*, and three French battleships in the area. These attacks caused a complete change in the system of naval action, anchorage, and supply. The navy withdrew to Mudros, and morale ashore plummeted.

The submarine presence in the Dardanelles theatre adversely affected maritime transport for sick and wounded from Gallipoli, as the vulnerable black ships followed the navy's withdrawal. From then, these vessels operated mainly after dusk. During daylight black ships had to be loaded outside the fire zone. There were immediate implications for Australian medical units on Gallipoli, as there was a corresponding increase in the holding time for casualties in field ambulances and the CCS.

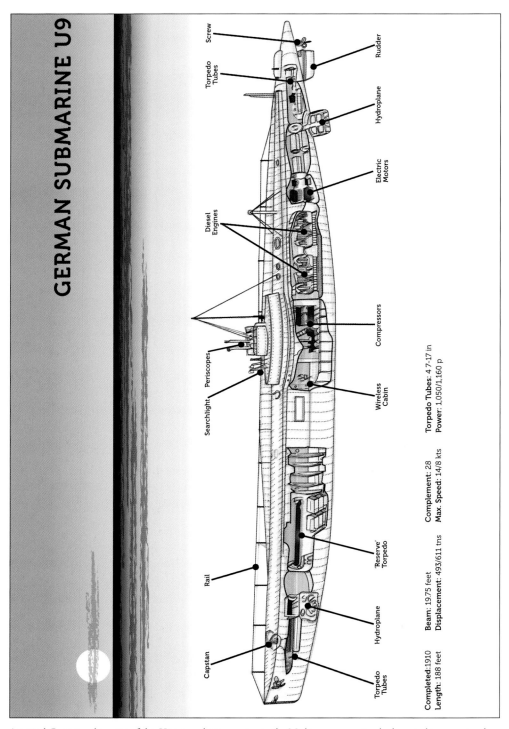

GERMAN SUBMARINE U9

Screw

Rudder

Torpedo Tubes

Hydroplane

Electric Motors

Diesel Engines

Compressors

Wireless Cabin

Searchlight, Periscopes

'Reserve' Torpedo

Rail

Hydroplane

Capstan

Torpedo Tubes

Completed: 1910
Length: 188 feet

Beam: 19.75 feet
Displacement: 493/611 tns

Complement: 28
Max. Speed: 14/8 kts

Torpedo Tubes: 4 7-17 in
Power: 1,050/1,160 p

A typical German submarine of the *U9* type, whose presence in the Mediterranean seriously disrupted transport and evacuation schedules.

It was not that strenuous efforts were lacking to rectify matters aboard hospital transports, but authorities could only use what ships were available. The alternative was to risk a build up of casualties on shore. Of necessity, the lesser of the two evils was chosen. Evacuations from Gallipoli sometimes had to be carried out in spite of serious shortages of medical staff to look after those on board. This was one aspect of medical evacuation which senior British medical officers underestimated.

An insight into life on board an improvised hospital ship in July comes from Sister Valerie Woniarski of No. 1 ASH. This ship had been hastily fitted out by sub-contractors, and among other problems it had defective plumbing. She wrote that there were awful swarms of flies, which made life hard for the patients on board. There was no pharmacist aboard, and even the most basic surgical appliances were in short supply.

The ship's galley was the only place where instruments could be sterilised, as each ward had only one Primus stove for this purpose, and most were out of order. There were only six nurses on board, so each nurse worked from 16 to 18 hours a shift. She added that the 'loss of thirty-nine cases before we reached port was partly due to the severity of their wounds, but also to the intense heat below decks'.

Even in August there were insufficient qualified medical personnel to staff the ships, to nurse both Australian and British casualties. This was no surprise, given that the total number of casualties removed on 7 August amounted to approximately 3800; on 8 August, 4100; on 9 August, 4200; and on 10 August, 3600. So bad was the shortage of staff that Lieutenant-Colonel Thomas Martin, commanding No. 2 ASH, received an urgent request that all convalescent patients in his hospital who were fit for such duty proceed to Britain as nursing attendants on various ships.

On the few occasions when reports of obvious administrative blunders did find their way to higher HQ, the results could be interesting. To illustrate this point, there is the case of the *Saturnia* in late August. One of Hamilton's staff officers was informed by the Roman Catholic chaplain aboard this ship, which was loaded with ammunition, that it had 800 sick and wounded aboard, with only two doctors to look after them.

According to Captain William Fraser of the 2nd LH Fd Amb, he and 12 men of his unit were ordered on 28 August to proceed to the *Saturnia*. He was told to prepare the ship to received 600 to 700 wounded. At 0700 the next day, 570 British wounded from Cape Helles were literally dumped aboard from the *Prince Abbas*.

Another medical officer, Major A.C. Purchas, a New Zealander, estimated the figure at closer to 1100. He surmised that the wounded were sent to *Saturnia* as the result of a mistaken radio signal. His story, although graphic, is not untypical of many shipboard medical scenes in those days. While he was on the upper deck he dressed 'a man who had about the largest wound I have ever seen, his whole back being laid open, and he was simply crawling with maggots'.

Wemyss later came on board, and was so shocked that he asked Purchase how he could help. We do not know Purchase's response, but Wemyss ordered every warship in Mudros to send a surgeon. At the time *Saturnia* was less than a kilometre from Hamilton's own HQ ship *Aragon*. The wounded were eventually transhipped to the *Nile* and *Minnewaska*, before being evacuated to Egypt. GHQ called for an immediate inquiry into why that had been allowed to happen, given that there were three hospital ships at Cape Helles.

TRANSPORT TO BASE HOSPITALS

No. 1 AGH had been in Cairo since January, and it became the bulwark for the Australian medical services in Egypt, both while the AIF was in training there, and well into 1916. Its registrar later wrote that the rapid expansion of this unit was undertaken entirely by a staff originally intended to care for the standard 520-bed establishment. Not until mid-June did medical reinforcements arrive, and the hospital received only a portion of those.

Most hospital accommodation in Cairo was improvised. Many large former hotels were commandeered for military use, although such was the influx in May that hundreds of AIF casualties were nursed in a boarded-over skating rink and in a joinery. For a time hundreds were placed outdoors for lack of accommodation. An idea of the growth of the No 1 AGH is indicated by its sub unit locations:

Helipolis Palace Hotel	1000 beds
Luna Park	1650
Atelier	450
Sporting Club	1250
Choubra Infectious Hospital	250
Abbassia Infectious Hospital	1250
Venereal Diseases, Abbassia	2000
Al Hayat, Helouan (Convalescent)	1250

As early as March, Williams cabled to Australia, pleading for the immediate addition of 20 medical officers, 25 NCOs, and 230 nurses and ORs. The solution proposed by the Defence Department in Melbourne was to use reinforcements who were already *en route* to Egypt and allocated to various units. The Australian Government had no real idea what were appropriate (medical) staffing numbers for the AIF.

When the first of the April wounded arrived in Cairo, No. 2 AGH (which arrived in Egypt with the first AIF convoy and had set up at the Mena House Hotel) was in the process of moving its establishment to another hotel.

The Heliopolis Palace Hotel, Cairo. The five-star facade belies its inadequacies as a hospital (AWM A03074)

Before a robust system was established in Egypt for dealing with incoming casualties, things were chaotic. It was a rude awakening for the Australian staff (who numbered at this time 28 officers, 92 nurses and 216 ORs) at No.1 AGH. On 29 April, without notice or warning of any kind, train loads of wounded began to arrive in large numbers. On 30 April and 1 May no fewer than 1352 cases were admitted.

Due to the chaos previously described, the hospitals were filled with slightly injured soldiers who should never have left Gallipoli. Private Brian Rainsford, a medic serving in Cairo, wrote that nearly all of the casualties who arrived on 30 April had minor wounds.

The system, or lack of it, was completely beyond the control of the AAMC, and there were other participants who could only look on and wring their hands. The military governor of Malta (850 kilometres from Lemnos), where several hospitals had been specially prepared, advised Hamilton that Malta had facilities ready to receive casualties, but ships full of wounded were still sent directly to Egypt.

Red Cross and other civilian volunteers who assisted on the wharves at Alexandria began asking probing questions, and were writing home about the 'scandalous' conditions. To be fair to the military authorities, they had little understanding of how completely the original medical plan had been crippled because the landing had not obtained its objectives, and because the terrain on Gallipoli meant that little hospital accommodation or wheeled transport could be set up or used ashore.

The diagram below provides an appreciation of some of the difficulties involved in evacuating sick and wounded to the base hospitals in Cairo. It shows the distribution systems in Egypt itself, as these affected AAMC units.

Disembarkation, Alexandria, May 1915. (Wellcome Library, London, L0032626B00)

Once at the wharves at Alexandria, casualties were transferred by motor or horse ambulances to hospital trains or to local hospitals. The days immediately following 25 April saw more than 16,000 wounded men enter Egypt, most of whom were admitted to hospitals in Cairo. The diagram on page 91 is based on a sketch by Sergeant O.P. Kenny of the 3rd Fd Amb. It shows how he understood the evacuation system to work.

There were scenes of much activity in Cairo after both the April landing and the August Offensive. Cath McNaughton, a nursing sister at No.1 AGH, wrote in her diary that the night she and other nurses arrived at the Ghezireh Palace Hotel on 13 August, 800 Gallipoli casualties, many of them seriously wounded, were admitted from fleets of motor ambulances from 1100 that night until 0300 the next day.

Alexandria and Cairo were not unique in receiving little, if any, advance warning of the arrival of casualties. Even in July, medical authorities on Malta were still expressing frustration at the poor coordination of the whole evacuation procedure. The island, as a key strategic base for the Mediterranean Fleet, had a number of excellent hospitals, and a large number of military barracks. With the troops on active service, these had been converted to accommodate casualties. However, their medical staffs were taken unawares by hospital or transport ships arriving to discharge their human cargoes with almost no notice.

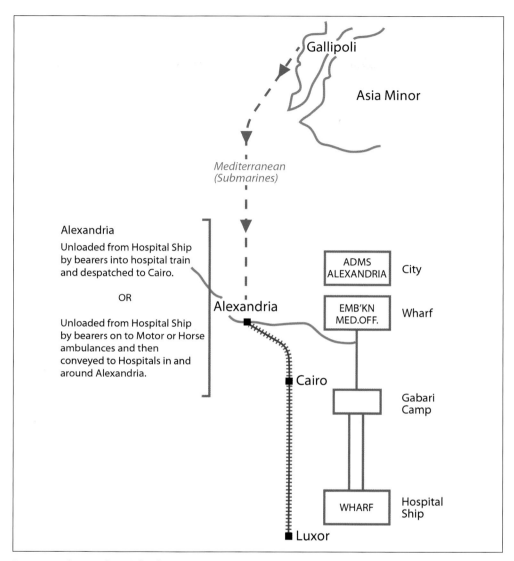

Evacuation schematic from Gallipoli to Egypt.

By late July some senior medical authorities were at last aware of the realities of a lengthy and complex campaign on Gallipoli. Babtie, in contrast to Ford's 'wait and see' policy, realised the need to increase hospital accommodation in Egypt and Malta, and put in place appropriate notification procedures.

In Cairo Ford appears to have followed a plan in which each problem was met as it came along, without any forward planning. In a letter to Brigadier-General C.R. McGrigor, HQ, Cairo, dated 22 April 1915, Ford shows this unpreparedness:

> The hospital ships on arrival at Alexandria will come under the orders of the G.O.C. in Chief, Egypt, and the disposal of all sick and wounded on board will be carried out

with the knowledge and approval of the D.M.S. in Egypt. Sick and wounded arriving from overseas may have to be accommodated in various hospitals in Egypt and even Civil hospitals as well if necessary, and this can only be done through a centralised authority ...

Hamilton advised Ford in July of a casualty estimate for the forthcoming August Offensive of 20,000. At that time there were about 18,000 hospital beds in Egypt, of which 10,000 were occupied, and Malta was preparing 10,000 beds, of which 5600 were then occupied. As the actual casualties from the August fighting totalled almost 30,000 by September, the entire hospital and evacuation system for the Gallipoli campaign almost collapsed for the second time.

A horse drawn ambulance with wounded aboard arriving at No. 2 Australian General Hospital (formerly the Mena House Hotel), Cairo. (AWMJ02139)

A conference in late September between senior navy and army medical and logistics officers came to a sobering conclusion. Even if no further military operations took place on Gallipoli, and assuming there were no reinforcements for the MEF, and that the normal rate of sick and wounded did not exceed 800 a day, medical evacuation could only just be carried out if the huge liner *Mauretania* (with accommodation for nearly 2000 patients) was added to the existing fleet of hospital ships. She did come into service, but not until late November.

Despite the urgency, the response was slow. Beds continued to be filled by sick and wounded until, on 4 August, the entire allied hospital accommodation in the Mediterranean had reached capacity. The only solution was to load large ocean liners, and transport patients directly to Britain. This method of evacuation was employed intermittently from August until the final withdrawal from Gallipoli in December.

For most of the Gallipoli campaign evacuating casualties from the front, particularly to base hospitals, became something of a vicious circle. The more casualties sustained on the peninsula, the more hospital ships were required to move them. But these same hospital ships were required to empty the base hospitals to Britain and Australia as the hospital population in Egypt and Malta swelled in proportion to the increase in the number of casualties.

Australian medical personnel could play only a small role in caring for their countrymen. The relative helplessness of the medical services was exacerbated when the MEF was visited by that other horseman of the Apocalypse, disease.

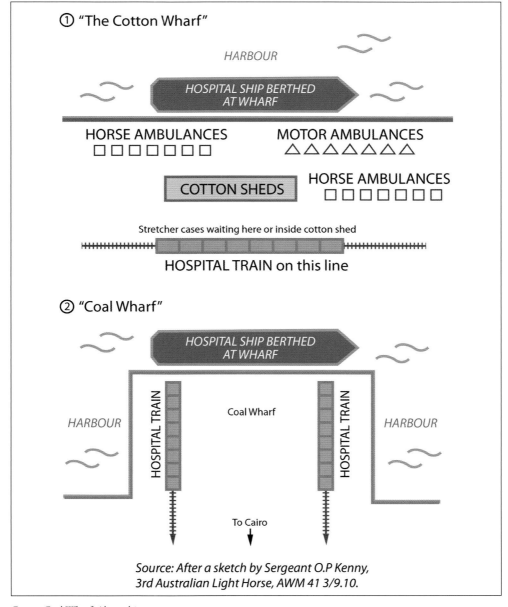

① "The Cotton Wharf"

HARBOUR

HOSPITAL SHIP BERTHED AT WHARF

HORSE AMBULANCES

MOTOR AMBULANCES

COTTON SHEDS

HORSE AMBULANCES

Stretcher cases waiting here or inside cotton shed

HOSPITAL TRAIN on this line

② "Coal Wharf"

HOSPITAL SHIP BERTHED AT WHARF

HOSPITAL TRAIN

Coal Wharf

HOSPITAL TRAIN

HARBOUR

HARBOUR

To Cairo

Source: After a sketch by Sergeant O.P Kenny, 3rd Australian Light Horse, AWM 41 3/9.10.

Cotton Coal Wharf, Alexandria.

CHAPTER 6:

The Other Enemy

Diseases flourish where sanitation cannot be implemented and supervised; this allows the rise of disease carriers or vectors. On Gallipoli, the principal culprit was the fly. Once disease gained a foothold, it had to be identified, its victims treated, and survivors protected from further ravages by preventative measures.

The costs of disease to the military, not only in terms of personnel losses, but also its effect on combat effectiveness, have to be considered. This factor is largely ignored when we think of this campaign and what it meant for Australia. In all these aspects the activities and influence of the AAMC played a crucial part.

After the Crimean War, military medicine advanced considerably in its understanding of diseases and their causes. This knowledge, however, was still confined to medical textbooks. Among the MEF's senior command there was insufficient awareness of the most effective preventative measures.

The losses from disease during the Boer War should have been in the minds of many of them. Only after disabling diseases had made huge inroads into the ranks, directly threatening the entire Gallipoli expedition, did GHQ listen to its medical advisors.

TABLE 2.2:
DEATHS PER THOUSANDS OF 'EXPOSED TO RISK' AMONG A.I.F OVERSEAS DURING 1915

	AIF	BOER WAR
Enteric Fevers	2.32	18.06
Dysentery	1.19	3.02
Diarrhea	0.12	0.05
Other 'Intestinal'	0.17	0.05
Other 'Infections'	5.00	0.20
Other Diseases	2.28	3.20
All Diseases	11.68	24.58
Died of Wounds	38.69	3.92
Killed in Action	113.65	9.59
TOTAL DEATHS	164.02	38.09

Source: AWM 27, 376.04[6].

Some of the more prescient staff officers, and others with service in the Boer War (such as Howse), did appreciate the ramifications of poor hygiene, and the importance of keeping disease at bay. Others who had served in South Africa (Hamilton among them) appear to have ignored these lessons. Still, for all the slaughter, World War I generally, and Gallipoli in particular, were vast improvements on the Boer War in terms of losses from disease.

In the Dardanelles theatre, disease meant both personnel wastage and a substantially increased workload for those AAMC personnel who remained on duty, even after the fighting had evolved to siege warfare and battle casualties declined. The overburdened hospitals at Lemnos were swamped with sick men by September.

To add to the troubles of the AAMC in Egypt, fresh troops arriving from Australia brought with them diseases, some infectious. Due to inadequate sanitation, accommodation, and inoculation in training camps in Australia, a number of men arrived in Egypt suffering from influenza, mumps and measles.

Venereal disease (VD) also featured prominently in health statistics among Australian reinforcements. VD constituted a significant nuisance factor for the AAMC, not only because it had to treat those afflicted, but because it also had to find accommodation and nursing staff to care for VD patients. The incidence of VD in the AIF simply reflected the male civilian population of Australia at the time. Its incidence in post-Federation Australia would surprise many nowadays.

SANITATION

Although the least glamorous, one of the vital functions of any medical service is to superintend and advise on sanitary measures and preventative strategies. The importance of this function had certainly been highlighted in South Africa 15 years earlier. The *Manual of Elementary Military Hygiene* (1912) stated that in the Boer War, for every man admitted to hospital with wounds, 17 were admitted because of disease.

The AAMC found that undue responsibility was placed on it for the propagation of sanitary measures at Anzac, responsibility that belonged to divisions, brigades and individual units. Engineers were used heavily, particularly in the construction of permanent latrines and drains, and to some extent this moved the onus further away from the combatant units really responsible for field sanitation.

Most infantry units were routinely delinquent when it came to keeping their lines clean. There was apathy, too, among the Diggers, despite their ranks thinning out as a direct result of poor hygiene. Combatant officers later realised that it was in their best interest to enforce the sanitary regulations that were circulated after the landing as part of routine orders. However, this realisation took many months of prodding from medical officers and NCOs, and the loss of combatant power in decimated infantry brigades.

Comprehensive sanitary measures on Gallipoli were relegated to the lowest priority until almost too late. Birrell should have been fortunate in the arrival in July of an official sanitation officer, Lieutenant-Colonel A.R. Aldridge, but he sent this officer away, because he considered Aldridge was not required. Aldridge then remained in limbo for more than five weeks before being used in his professional capacity.

The ferocity of the first attacks, together with the terrain at Anzac, worked against the organisation of sanitation until mid-May. The situation deteriorated so quickly in the confined space of the area of operations, however, that military police were brought in to oversee sanitation with the strong enforcement arm these measures required at that time.

The month of May was enough time to establish breeding grounds for insects. Flies, and later lice, were the bane of medical staff, and the cause of much sickness and discomfort. Insects featured prominently in soldiers' letters and diaries. One bemused soldier wrote home that in:

> the insect line we could count quite a tidy little collection … We had flies by the hundred billion. They were everywhere, from the heaps of dead to the cooks' pots. Put jam on a biscuit and it was always a sprint between you and the flies, the event usually ending in a dead heat.

After the April landings, men were picked from infantry units to look after the cleanliness of their own lines. Rubbish, and the unavoidable spillage of foodstuffs and grain from the two divisional supply depots on the beach, attracted flies that bred profusely. At that time refuse was put into tubs near the beach, and dumped at sea.

Despite the pleas of medical officers, initially rubbish was not burnt for tactical reasons, as smoke attracted enemy fire. However, incinerators were operational by the end of May in the immediate HQ area at Anzac Cove.

On 4 May Howse formed a 'sanitation company' of about 30 men, obtained from various units behind the lines. He organised it into three sections of eight or nine men under NCOs, each operating in part of the 1st Division's area. It fell to these men to dig the necessary latrines and keep the ground, especially near wells, free of rubbish and other debris. However (unlike at Cape Helles), there was no professional sanitary unit operating at Anzac until 13 August. There simply weren't enough men.

With the growth in the fly population at the end of May, there was a corresponding increase in diarrhoea (often incorrectly diagnosed as dysentery). But there was at that time no medical officer able to isolate the cause. With the warmer weather, and in an attempt to stop an increase of illness, the AAMC sent out numerous memoranda to the troops about basic sanitary regulations.

It was not long before the fly menace and other health hazards began to attract attention from senior officers. By mid-May, even officers from the general staff of the ANZAC observed soldiers using precious springs for washing, and washing in buckets close to the water and fouling it. Latrines had not been filled in, and apart from the stench of rotting corpses and unwashed bodies, flies were gathering in discarded tins with food still in them. The insects bred in plague proportions.

Corporal Eugene Kitson of the 4th Fd Amb wrote in his diary that flies:

> soon became our worst enemy, starting about the middle of May and becoming unbearable about the middle of June, bringing in their train dysentery and enteric fever. The dysentery became very prevalent about the middle of June and swelled the sick parade enormously, sometimes the number of [men at] sick parades totalled 200.

Operations frequently had to be curtailed because of the combination of dust and flies. Combatant officers only then became alert to the problem. Sickness was also an important military consideration, as the period of convalescence for dysentery victims, for example, was three months.

Latrines continued to constitute a major health hazard. The commander of the 2nd Fd Amb noted that 'Closed latrines are scattered everywhere and for those in use there is no means of protecting them from flies'. The shortage of suitable materials, such as wood and tin, was such that this problem was not adequately addressed until the campaign was almost over. The first improvised fly-proof latrines were built by a sergeant of engineers just before the Lone Pine battle, and were constructed from the timber of wrecked boats that had broken up on the beach.

The only bright spot in an otherwise dismally unhygienic environment was the proximity of accessible, if dangerous, beaches for bathing. Given the shortage of water, this was the only means by which Diggers could wash. Swimming also provided a much-needed break and exercise for the men. Despite constant casualties from Turkish small arms and shrapnel fire, the Australian and New Zealand commanders did nothing to stop this activity, probably because such a directive would have been impossible to enforce. Despite the death around them, members of the medical services retained their sense of humour and would write about 'mixed bathing' - men and bullets.

On Lemnos it was some time before the island's sanitation was anything more than rudimentary, despite to the presence of several large military hospitals. The lack of pre-planning, shortages of building and engineering materials, and the ubiquitous lack of small boats to get such materials to shore were to blame. Even when matters did improve, the hospitals there still used very basic measures to prevent infection and to avoid disease outbreaks. There were large incinerators which burnt up all refuse, and in the hospitals' infectious wards chloride of lime, or creosol solution, was sprinkled on the floor or ground two or three times a day.

Lack of space and continued fighting worked against the early establishment of a comprehensive and satisfactory sanitary system at Anzac. Nor, at the time, were the vitamin deficiencies (particularly B and C) of the monotonous army diet sufficiently understood or addressed. The results were costly. The increased workload for a progressively decimated medical service also became an important consideration in the decision to abandon Gallipoli.

DISEASES

There was a great amount of sickness on Gallipoli from June 1915, and the diseases that concerned the AAMC most were dysentery, typhoid, jaundice, and influenza. The changing seasons played an important part in the relative prominence of each. Many sick troops were not correctly diagnosed at the time, and hundreds of troops diagnosed as suffering from debilitating diarrhoea actually had dysentery.

Strategic demands ensured that the AAMC was basically in a no-win situation. Commanders were increasingly impatient at convalescent troops being retained in hospitals on Lemnos and in Egypt. As the campaign progressed, and more and more soldiers became ill, the pressure to retain unfit Diggers at the front also mounted. Naturally, retaining such cases at the front increased the spread of infection.

Cooks of the 1st Australian Field Ambulance serving a 'light diet' meal to walking sick. (AWM A01805)

To better appreciate how badly the AIF was affected by disease, mention should be made of Colonel Sir James Purves-Stewart, Consulting Physician to the MEF. Immediately after his arrival on Imbros on 8 September this officer, an experienced London specialist, made enquiries as to the ratio of sickness among the various forces then deployed on the Gallipoli peninsula. After studying this data, he concluded that the proportion of sick was markedly different among the three forces. None of the medical officers on the peninsula had identified this fact.

He brought a fresh perspective to the matter, and came to a new and somewhat startling conclusion. This concerned the physical condition of the men who had not reported sick, but who were still in the firing trenches as front-line troops. Purves-Stewart made a three-day study of the Diggers on Gallipoli, and he knew that some of them (such as those at Anzac Cove) had been under almost continuous fire, or the threat of fire, for over four and a half months.

Unlike on the Western Front or in Turkish units deployed on the peninsula, there had been no rotation of units to the rear. Troops at Anzac were therefore presenting with an abnormally high percentage of sick, three or four times as high as troops a few kilometres south at Cape Helles.

TABLE 2.3: THESE PERCENTAGES REFER ONLY TO TROOPS WHO WERE ON ACTIVE DUTY, NOT THOSE 'OFF SICK'.

PERCENTAGE OF SICK EVACUATED	WEEK ENDING 28 AUGUST	WEEK ENDING 5 SEPTEMBER
Helles (About 30,000 Troops)	4.4%	5.1%
Suvla (About 26,000 Troops)	1.9%	1.7%
Anzac (About 30,000 Troops)	6.6%	7.5%

Source: Personal narrative of Colonel Sir James Purves-Stewart, Consulting Physician to the Forces.
AWM 41 Butler Papers (Box 4) File No. 4/62.

The table clearly shows the difference in health between soldiers at Anzac and troops in other areas on Gallipoli. Purves-Stewart wrote that the:

contrast between the old and the fresh troops was striking. The older troops were emaciated in 77 [percent] of cases. 64 [percent] of these men were suffering from indolent ulcers of the skin, chiefly of the hands and shins. A large proportion, 78 [percent], had occasional diarrhoeal attacks. Most striking of all was the rapidity and feebleness of the heart's action.

The medical name at that time for this condition was Disordered Action of the Heart, or effort syndrome, a vague term incorporating everything from asthma to what was called 'anxiety neurosis'.

After doing nothing on the matter for a full five months, Hamilton was stirred by Purves-Stewart's report. Steps were taken to improve general health by rotating the men off the peninsula for a rest. Moves were also made to introduce canteens, from which soldiers could buy fresh rations, fruit and sweets.

The difference in the health of soldiers at Anzac and those elsewhere on the peninsula was due to three factors. First, the lack of variety in the army ration (bully beef, tea, biscuits and jam) must have lowered the men's resistance to infection. Second was the absence of any respite from a dangerous and highly stressful front-line environment. Such exposure may have made Diggers prone to illnesses that might not have occurred had they been able to exercise and enjoy some recreation. A third element may have been the more intensive battle fatigue suffered by those at Anzac, although British troops at Cape Helles had to operate in a similar environment.

To appreciate how this situation arose, let us return to the beginning of the campaign. The fly menace has already been noted. Flies were the chief means by which bacillary dysentery and amoebic dysentery (which had been brought from Egypt) spread. The difference between these is that symptoms of the former develop more quickly and are more severe. Jaundice started to occur in August, had replaced dysentery in significance by October, and by the end of the campaign had reached epidemic proportions. While fly breeding went largely unchecked, dysentery and infectious intestinal diseases generally became rife.

In September orders were given to treat every case of dysentery with emetine, but No. 4 Advanced Depot of Medical Stores at Anzac possessed neither emetine, nor needles for its injection. One can only speculate what proportion of sick men during those months had dysentery, and what proportion diarrhoea. Typhus and cholera (which did not occur at Gallipoli) were common in the Turkish part of the Mediterranean. Typhus is an infectious disease carried by the body louse, of which there was no shortage in the cramped conditions of the trenches at Anzac.

Paratyphoid was another problem. According to one medical authority, paratyphoid fever (so called because the symptoms were less severe than ordinary typhoid) was more prevalent on Gallipoli and Lemnos, where it was ten times as common as typhoid fever. For the MEF as a whole he quotes 5700 cases of enteric fever that occurred among the 96,683 medical casualties of the 300,000 men who fought on Gallipoli up to the middle of December 1915. The AAMC was impotent in the face of the unknown, and the sense of helplessness can be gauged from the unit diary of the 7th Fd Amb in November. It recorded that many of its men appeared to be suffering from typhoid or paratyphoid, but no one knew how they had contracted it.

Diarrhoea was common to all of the intestinal diseases at Gallipoli. As a medic, James McPhee could with authority write: 'With the cold it's an experience for the unfortunates with bowel complaints to have to go down at night from the dug-outs to the low ground, and sit on an ice cold latrine pole: the close "psst" at intervals of a stray bullet makes company welcome, and visits as brief as possible'.

Initially, these men were evacuated because they were of no use in the trenches. As sick lists grew and reinforcements were similarly afflicted, however, more and more sick were kept at Anzac, often in special dugouts at the dressing stations. There they were rested and placed on a 'soft' diet, when suitable food supplies could be obtained. Each medical officer did what he could in the circumstances.

Major Arthur Butler, the 9th Battalion's RMO, opted for a system under which a medic had a special dugout, and did nothing but prepare invalid foods – sago, rice, cornflour, porridge etc., to which milk was added. Any Digger with diarrhoea was given a slip on which was written 'light duties' and the number of days 'sick leave'. Butler then signed and dated it. While the symptoms might have been addressed, the cause remained. Unfortunately, the period of convalescence for typhoid fever was about six months, and such a long period of absence had serious consequences for the military effort.

Some soldiers were inoculated for cholera aboard troopships *en route* to Egypt, and not a few received a second dose, but Hamilton vetoed compulsory inoculation for Imperial troops. Nonetheless, the AIF for its part undertook an inoculation program for cholera, typhoid and smallpox. By 16 July Howse reported that 4000 Australian troops had been vaccinated. While outbreaks of cholera were reported in Asiatic Turkey, there were no cases on Gallipoli in 1915.

Half way through the campaign, fatigue and poor diet caught up with the 'original' Diggers, who then succumbed easily to sickness. A New Zealand staff officer later recalled that by September, troops weakened by continuous hardships and malnutrition were easy prey to dysentery and similar ailments.

The Australian trench system, at least in the early months at Anzac, was a health hazard. Open latrines, fly-blown corpses and poor sanitation led to an increase in disease. (Jeff Isaacs)

Average daily sick parades

Average daily sick parades of an RMO of the 3rd Brigade, shown by weeks as a percentage of battalion strength

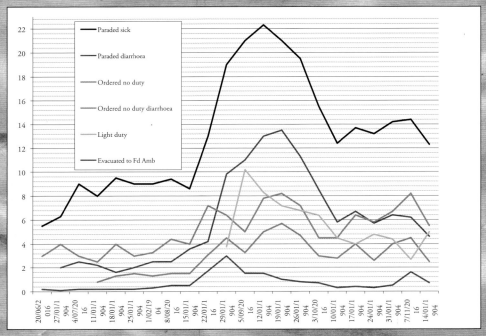

The weekly rate (percent of weekly average strength) of men from the 1st Australian Division (12,000 troops) evacuated from Anzac for sickness and wounds

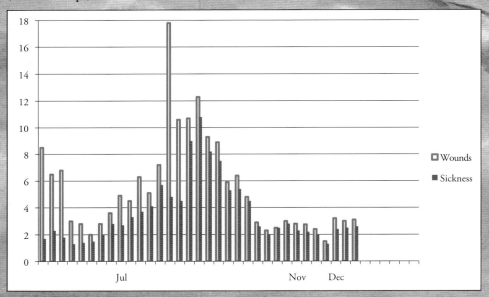

Medical units were also kept busy with men troubled by septic sores. These developed after men were scratched by the prickly scrub, or meat or jam tins, and were healed only with great difficulty.

The war diaries of medical units chronicle not only the prominence of disease, but also the increase in different types of sickness. This increase was a function of the length of time men stayed at Anzac (during which their health deteriorated), as well as the weather. In the month of July, one field ambulance had an average of 67 men a day attend its sick parades.

After August respiratory diseases, loosely grouped under influenza, were added to dysenteric diarrhoea. September saw a peak in the incidence of infectious diseases. Fevers of unknown origin became the prevailing sickness, while typhoid was still worrying medical authorities, as many medical personnel fell sick while they cared for soldiers suffering from it.

The picture painted in official diaries was bleak. For the month of October, the 5th Fd Amb admitted 73 wounded and 857 sick men; while it successfully returned 331 men to their units, a further 532 patients had to be evacuated. Between August and November the 6th Fd Amb treated 896 wounded and 2108 sick. Of these 1857 were evacuated, and 909 men were returned to their units.

IMPLICATIONS – MILITARY AND MEDICAL

The implications for combatant units at Anzac were clear, and commanders had to consider these statistics in any plan for offensive operations. With the coming of cold weather in December, the sick parade profile changed to include influenza, jaundice, and trench foot.

From July, medical reports from commanders and medical committees were unanimous in their recognition of a decimated soldiery, and signalled ominous portents for the next few months, particularly the winter. Many troops had been on continuous active duty since 25 April, had fought in numerous engagements, and were constantly subjected to the physical and psychological stress of combat. There had been no relief in terms of rest, or change of diet or routine, and reinforcements had been few.

Most troops were suffering from diarrhoea, and were physically and mentally exhausted. AAMC units suffered as well, and in their diaries many doctors and orderlies complained of feeling weak. Struggling in the face of declining staff numbers, the AAMC was hard pressed to cope, which increased the pressure to evacuate sick men offshore, where they could be properly looked after in hospitals, and above all in cases of infectious disease, isolated.

As the troops collectively underwent a metamorphosis from the sturdy, bronzed physiques of legend to staggering, emaciated men, barely able in some cases to hold a rifle, it became obvious to their commanders that countermeasures could no longer be postponed. Medical personnel worked amid pathetic scenes, and wrote of men fainting during sick parades.

Bedford also noted in his diary the poor health of the troops at Anzac, and recommended that units of the 1st Division be moved to a rest camp. As a result, a special commission of experts visited Anzac and recommended a more varied diet, improved sanitation, and better protection of water wells. Significantly, and perhaps inexplicably, it did not recommend rest camps.

Those worst afflicted, the rank and file in the front lines, left vivid accounts of their own observations. By August the men were in a bad state, as one soldier wrote:

> Before the Lone Pine affair they were bad enough but the last few days here have completely broken them up. It is piteous, really to see them. Great hulking fellows or at least the remains of them crawling about doubled up with internal pain due to dysentery, lying down utterly exhausted every hundred yards they go, others masses of septic sores.

The toll was heavy and the tactical implications were serious. A member of the 4th Light Horse Regiment wrote that 'Of the original squadron that left Victoria 150 strong we have two officers and sixty-nine men left and only half of them are fit for duty now'.

The poor conditions continued to take their toll on the AAMC. In September alone, the 2nd Fd Amb lost 40 of its men evacuated sick. They were joined in the following month by another 52 staff, all evacuated sick. If the Ottoman army had made a determined advance at this time, it is highly questionable if the Anzac positions would have held.

On 23 August, Hamilton cabled to the War Office that the average net wastage from sickness and battle was 24 percent of the fighting strength of his force per month. On the previous day Bedford recommended (for a second time) that some of the 1st Division be moved to a rest camp, but this was stalled through lack of reinforcements. Imbros had already been used as a rest camp in July; the average stay of Diggers at that time was four days. By September the period had been extended to four weeks.

From 7 September wider relief was possible, after the arrival of brigades from the 2nd Division. The 1st, 2nd and 4th Brigades left for a well-earned rest at a new camp established at Sarpi, at West Mudros. Subsequently the 1st and 2nd Fd Ambs were relieved by the 6th, while the 4th Fd Amb deployed to Lemnos after being relieved by the 7th.

On 20 September Colonel John Monash (then commanding the 4th Brigade) wrote home from Mudros:

> Since last writing the declining health of the troops became daily more acute, and so at last the higher command, from sheer force of circumstances, was compelled to consent to a withdrawal of five of the brigades which have done the lion's share of the fighting up to now.

This contrasted with the Turkish practice, where on a periodic basis units were pulled out of the line and sent to rest camps some ten to 15 kilometres to the rear.

Charles Bean wrote that there was a justifiable fear that if an officer or man became separated from his unit at the front, however short the time, there was no telling when he would return to it. This greatly increased the desire of all responsible commanders to keep their sick at Anzac, and that of many of the sick themselves to stay there from a sense of duty to their mates. This also presented a dilemma for the medical services. Should seriously ill soldiers, especially those suffering from infectious diseases, be treated (and retained) at the front, or should they be sent to proper medical care, but in the process possibly be lost for weeks or even months?

The return of troops to their units was not helped by poor staff work in the AAMC. Many a soldier was evacuated in quiet times without proper documentation. This led to confusion, and was responsible for many casualties being lost to their units at the very time when the units could not obtain replacements.

The long periods of time spent by sick or wounded troops convalescing in Egypt, Malta or Britain was a sore point with many combatant officers. The chronic lack of seaborne transport prevented the speedy return of convalescents. On arriving at Mudros with his troops for a rest, Monash immediately sent selected officers to Alexandria, 'to round up' both convalescents and reinforcements.

Even on Lemnos AAMC units did not escape disease, and this made life more difficult for those left to treat and nurse the influx of sick from Gallipoli. The Australian hospital units in Cairo were equally prone to sickness and other occupational hazards, as were their counterparts on the peninsula, more so when they were nursing men with infectious diseases. A large percentage of doctors and hospital nursing and orderly staff could be off-duty at any time.

One of them wrote that the persistently hot climate, combined with overwork, the inability to take adequate exercise, and the added risk of disease inseparable from hospital life, had all taken their toll on hospital staff. As the Gallipoli campaign dragged on, other factors combined to add to their woes.

CHAPTER 7:

Unwanted Distractions

While less significant than disease, several other problems together contributed to the medical challenges faced on Gallipoli. The source of at least some of these problems, however, can be traced to Australia itself in 1914 and later.

The initial enlistment of unfit personnel, lack of water (crucial to medical procedures), and an inadequate diet proved continuous sources of anxiety to medical personnel. These eventually helped contribute to gastro-intestinal disease, including debilitating diarrhoea. Dental problems also sapped the strength of many soldiers, while medical units faced constant problems with the supply and distribution of medical and surgical supplies.

The AAMC was also blamed for keeping convalescents away from the trenches for too long, a criticism that, while partly justified, was largely beyond its control to rectify. Psychological problems of a type and scale not seen before also had to be dealt with by a wholly inexperienced medical staff.

ENLISTMENT OF UNFIT PERSONNEL

The results of inadequate physical screening of Diggers when they volunteered at home became apparent to medical units stretched to cope with the outbreak of influenza, bronchitis, mumps, measles and VD that occurred in the Australian camps in Egypt from January to March 1915.

Soon after World War I broke out, and as the Gallipoli campaign began, resources in Australia were stretched to breaking point as tens of thousands of volunteers were hurriedly put through basic military training. While their health was the responsibility of the AAMC, to a large extent civilian medical practitioners performed the initial medical examination of volunteers on behalf of the army and navy. The immediate benefits to the small medical staff of the AAMC which this system provided were outweighed by the haphazard procedures and ambiguous guidelines followed by many GPs (not all of whom were competent) in certifying unsuitable recruits as fit.

The strain these men placed during and after the Gallipoli campaign on the army generally, and the AAMC specifically, was considerable. Even before the first troop convoy left Australia in August 1914, 37 men were put ashore as 'medically unfit for active service'. Of these two were mentally ill, three had debilitating middle-ear disease, while another two suffered from epilepsy.

Other unfit troops, who were enlisted only because of negligent civilian recruiting doctors in Australia, reached Egypt undetected. To some extent Australian doctors were steamrolled in 'medical examinations' performed during the initial months of the war, when thousands flocked to enlist. However, the Defence Department took no steps to ensure even random follow-up physical examinations by army doctors.

WATER

Although there were potable wells on Gallipoli, these could never supply the needs of such a large body of troops; there were early scenes of thirsty men cutting canvas hoses that brought water from flat-bottomed boats to troughs on the beaches. During the period from April almost until the December evacuation, Anzac troops had to rely on water coming from as far afield as Britain and Egypt. The Cape Helles sector further south was more fortunate in having access to several wells.

A large new oil tanker full of water was brought to Imbros from Port Said. This vessel was then refilled by the constant coming and going of smaller tankers between Mudros and the waterworks in Egypt. Transports arriving from Britain emptied their surplus water into this tanker before returning. The precariousness of the supply lines has already been noted, susceptible as they were to submarines, mines, storms, delays and mismanagement. The supply of water became an added headache for the military and medical authorities.

The scarcity of water on Gallipoli was a major problem for most of the campaign. It was directly responsible for a number of health problems, and was a contributing factor in several military failures, the Suvla Bay attack in August being the most noteworthy.

There was almost never sufficient water available for Diggers to drink, and from their meagre ration they were expected to cook their food and wash. According to one soldier, even when the fighting was at its most intense in the summer months 'the average ration of water for all purposes was, perhaps, at most, a pint and a half, sometimes only a pint'. The situation is illustrated by this signal to the 4th Battalion:

> Owing to the stress of circumstances the supply of water to troops in the trenches has become a very serious matter. Tomorrow the maximum amount of water which will be available per company [approximately 200 men] for all purposes will be eight tins [145.4 litres] … sufficient to make one lot of tea of about half pint per man.

Water was also essential for the proper functioning of medical units, as it was required for sterilising instruments, mixing solutions, irrigating wounds, and for cleaning. Often it was in such short supply that wounds had to be dressed using sea water. After the onset of disease in July, units sometimes found it difficult to muster sufficient men fit enough to go to the beach and undertake the long haul back to the trenches with tins of water.

During the first days of the landing, troops, horses and mules polluted the few streams on Anzac, rendering them useless. Fortunately there were no contamination problems either of water in the tankers or water coming from the wells at Anzac, as both sources were well guarded. This was just as well, because for a long time there were no water purification chemicals available in this theatre of war.

Despite the best efforts of both the navy and the army to improve the water supply, there were always problems. In May De Robeck, the naval commander at the Dardanelles, keenly aware of the lack of water for the troops ashore, calculated that 300 one ton tanks were needed.

The trouble was that almost as soon as these tanks were taken ashore, they were shelled by artillery. A similar fate overtook some large water condensers at Anzac Cove, which were soon found by Ottoman shells. The amphibious nature of the Gallipoli campaign caught the army unawares, as traditionally armies relied on rivers and established wells. Simply put, the MEF had no provision for storing water.

Members of the 1st Light Horse Regiment filling their water canteens from Furphy tanks in Shrapnel Gully. Note the beard, the variety of dress and the Red Cross on the rear tanker. (AWM A03127)

RATIONS

For the Gallipoli campaign as a whole, rations were usually of sufficient quantity, although the quality varied, and there is no doubt that rations almost never changed. However, some of the allies fared better than the AIF. French troops, for example, had access to better food and cooking methods. Many British troops had access to a greater supply and variety of rations. For the Australians, the same unvaried issue consumed over several months made the onset of health problems almost inevitable.

In April the field ration was adequate for fit troops, for whom the food was a change from shipboard rations. The weather was mild, sanitary problems had not yet arisen, and most Diggers were content with their food at this time. Beside the ordinary bully beef, the ration could occasionally include abundant corned mutton, tinned beef, onions, potatoes and tinned vegetables.

After May, however, when military stalemate set in, the weather became hotter, and transport of supplies became more precarious, soldiers soon became tired of the monotonous salt bully beef and hard biscuit. In July and August particularly, there were no adequate foods to give soldiers suffering from gastro-intestinal diseases. Both hospitals and field ambulances were greatly handicapped through lack of fresh foodstuffs. They had cases of tinned food and condensed milk, but some of that was of questionable quantity.

Most men cooked for themselves, as the nature of the terrain and the type of fighting often precluded organised mess arrangements. This contributed to the spread of gastro-intestinal infection, due both to the lack of water for washing utensils and the fly menace.

Depending on the tactical situation, unit cooks sometimes only provided tea. It was a moot point as to whether the 'tea' was the genuine thing, if Private T.W. Liddell of the 23rd Battalion is to be believed. He wrote of the tea that 'sometimes it isn't saturated with sugar, or spoilt with excess of milk; often too it makes one think of flood waters; never however do the flies refuse to bathe in it if left uncovered for a few seconds'.

The theory was that cooks could better supervise water rations. They were often the only men with official access to what firewood was available. Supervision of hygiene was difficult, as was proper storage of foodstuffs, which easily became contaminated by flies and dust, or went bad in the heat.

The latter was a common problem with fresh meat, which was often good Australian frozen beef, but by the time it had been landed and carried up the slopes, it was flyblown when it reached the trenches. For some, the standard ration could be supplemented by less orthodox means, as Private Victor Laidlaw related: 'we were very lucky today, in getting fresh fish, these fish are got by bombs, the concussion temporarily stuns them and you just wade into the sea and pick them up'.

Stories of poor provisioning, the non-appearance of foodstuffs from Australia, and the lack of canteen facilities, in conjunction with the increase in sickness among Australian troops, gave rise to much criticism at home. Bread was occasionally received by Australian troops, but it was often mouldy and made with dirty flour, and it was the subject of a number of medical reports. Apart from providing variety to the diet, fresh bread, according to one medical officer would 'be a Godsend for men with broken teeth and dentures of whom there are many'. It was becoming obvious to medical officers that a considerable amount of sickness was because of the monotony and lack of vitamins in the standard ration.

Eventually pressure began to be exerted through official channels. Late in August Hamilton received a telegram from the Secretary of State, which asked him to report on rations generally, their variety, and whether canteen stores sent from Britain in July and August had been received. He was also asked to explain 'the cause of debility of such an excessive number of men among the Australians'.

A comparison with how other troops fared at Gallipoli is helpful in assessing the situation in which the AAMC worked. The Turks appeared to exist on relatively basic fare, but were inured to it. There is a description of some Turks taken prisoner in June. Private G. Gower, a stretcher-bearer with the 15th Battalion, wrote that they 'were in an awful state. Old clothes, no water in their bottles, and they were only issued with 1 biscuit and 1 small onion to last them 24 hours'.

On the other hand our French allies, who were located in a better site, and possessed a well organised commissariat, were considerably better off overall than either the Diggers or the British. A French doctor wrote home to his wife that he lacked 'nothing. Corned beef abounds, also bread. There are potatoes, cold meat – mutton and beef – chocolate, rum …' The French also had a daily ration of red wine. A British soldier wrote home: 'On the whole, the French retained health and vigour best, their ration being less monotonous, and themselves more fastidious in cookery'.

Strenuous attempts were made to have a canteen sent to Anzac. There was ample precedent for such an establishment, as Hamilton noted in his diary. He had endeavoured to secure a canteen as early as May, and had asked the War Office for permission either to let him run a canteen locally on the lines of the South Africa Field Force, or let him run it himself.

By July other organisations, notably the Young Men's Christian Association (YMCA), the Australian Comforts' Fund (ACF), and to a lesser extent the Australian Red Cross, started to provide material support to the casualties and other patients of the AAMC. The ACF, founded in August 1914, was responsible for looking after the needs of soldiers commanded by a military or combatant commander, whereas the Red Cross cared for all men under medical care.

It was not until August, however, that the first ships carrying large supplies of canteen stores began to arrive. It was never enough, Hamilton noting that it was 'a mere flea bite of £10000 worth'. Birdwood had written to Hamilton telling him that the Australian doctors ascribed much sickness to the monotony of the diet. Journalist Charles Bean and every other Australian at Anzac made the same observation.

In September Howse disputed official British reports, which stated that supplies of rations to Australian troops were adequate, and he cited a number of supply returns that indicated severe inadequacies in the supply of fresh bread, vegetables and frozen meat. He also scotched a further criticism, which stemmed from a British supply depot, concerning the assumption that the abnormal amount of jam and molasses consumed by Australians contributed to the increase of diarrhoea. 'As no molasses has been issued to the 1st Aust. Div. it cannot have been a factor and I do not believe that well made jam could account for such a type of Dysenteric Diarrhoea that exists at Anzac.'

'In summer it was impossible to keep the flies, which had gorged on the dead, from getting into our food. An open jam tin was like an invitation to thousands of them to lunch with me.' (Jeff Isaacs)

It is not generally recognised that Australian medical units on Lemnos had to pay exorbitant prices to supplement the ration issue. The commanding officer of the 5th Fd Amb wrote that he had '110 patients in hospital – Have reported to the ADMS that eggs have not been procurable since Oct. 7th … It seems strange that although eggs are not procurable as a medical comfort, the men of my unit were able to purchase them at [a very expensive] two shillings per dozen'.

Diggers going to Lemnos were 'loaded with commissions and made the Greek traders rich by buying tinned figs, pineapples, and milk at fabulous prices …' Those coming from a well off country such as Australia were scandalised. 'The prices charged for things are enormous, it is a wonder the government does not do something to regulate the prices.' Both the Australian and British governments were slow to move, despite pleas from medical authorities.

The YMCA, working from Egypt, set up a bakery and a store on Imbros, and ran a daily shuttle service to Anzac with large consignments of cakes, buns, fresh fruit and vegetables. Their difficulty was trying to meet demand. Two weeks later they sailed to Gallipoli, and in September set up a YMCA 'depot' in Reserve Gully.

Both the Australian Red Cross and the ACF (neither of which had any official function) had insufficient personnel to ensure adequate distribution of goods once they arrived at Alexandria from Australia. Consequently, very little reached sick and wounded Australians actually on the Gallipoli peninsula.

TEETH

Another problem was dental hygiene. Many troops reached Egypt who should have been classed as unfit because of their teeth, or lack of them. The problem was made worse because the AAMC did not have even one dentist on its establishment, although some professional dentists were withdrawn from the ranks to do part-time palliative work. Many doctors noted that the standard of dental fitness was very low, which is unsurprising, as it reflected the poor national dental profile at the time.

Dental problems were a major source of difficulty for the AAMC and the AIF, and yet are rarely mentioned in the Gallipoli literature as being a source of serious concern. Men without teeth could not live on the rations provided, and they were sometimes sick with diseases hastened by inadequate dental hygiene. Such men were a drain on valuable medical time and facilities. Militarily they were unfit, and dental wastage was both a cause and effect of the rate of reinforcements on the peninsula.

This particular problem was, however, of Australia's own making. Initially lack of interest and rigid establishment codes, and later a want of equipment, caused this glaring shortcoming in the medical services. Before the Gallipoli campaign began Australian dentists tried to make the army aware of the problem, but to no avail. There was simply no provision in the army for dental treatment, and dentists who tried to enlist as such were refused, because they were not provided for in the (British) War Establishment, which the Australian military forces used.

While an AAMC Dental Reserve was formed in January 1915, no officer or technician appointments were made until March, and so these men did not become active at Anzac until later in the year. Before the AIF left Australia, Bridges asked the Defence Department to reconsider its refusal to send a dental team with the troops, noting that New Zealand had included dental officers in its contingent (although they were not issued with any instruments).

'I believe', Bridges wrote in one of his despatches, 'that the service of a dentist in the field would make for efficiency and economy as an alternative to the transfer of men to the base for treatment'. This observation was also the nub of the medical services problem. Combatant commanders were exasperated at losing their fighting men because they were sent away on account of problems with their teeth.

In June Babtie, the PDMS, correctly noted that for all their supposed physical prowess, Diggers had very bad teeth (as did most of the Australian population at that time), and many British soldiers also required dental treatment, as they had plates which got broken, either deliberately or accidentally. His solution was to have these problems fixed either on Gallipoli or at Imbros by dentists. This would stop a lot of invaliding and sending men to Egypt.

Howse had already approached Babtie to supply 20 dentists for the Australians, but Babtie was content to start with 20 for the entire MEF. Later, Howse tried again to resolve what was by then becoming an alarming problem, as many RMOs were reporting that men with serious dental problems were beginning to suffer from persistent dyspepsia and diarrhoea. They recovered while they were on an 'invalid diet', but as Howse pointed out, on return to ordinary rations these soldiers returned to the sick list, and were subsequently evacuated from Anzac. Howse wanted properly equipped dentists and dental assistants appointed, so that they could begin immediately on urgent work.

Despite relatively large numbers of medical officers and staff working in Egypt, the dental situation there was still poor. The local civilian dentists had been overwhelmed with military patients. Not a few men obtained emergency treatment from mates who had been dentists before enlisting.

Others simply suffered in silence, or were sent from Alexandria to Egypt or Malta, and not infrequently returned to Anzac having had no treatment whatever. 'There is considerable difficulty experienced now amongst our men of getting any dental attention ashore and especially where a man is wearing plates and breaks them.'

On 6 July the Australian Government authorised 'the appointment of fourteen dental officers, twelve mechanics and thirteen Privates for service in the AIF overseas'. Such reinforcements took time to materialise where they were needed most. Appointments were made from dentists in Australia and those serving abroad in various convalescent and medical units, but the supply of dental equipment continued to be a problem.

The AAMC, ever resourceful, did its best to adapt. Some ambulances and other medical units had a dentist and/or a dental mechanic within their ranks, working as medics. These were soon hard at work dealing with troops of their own brigades. One of these was a Sydney dentist, G. Douglas, who had enlisted as a private in the 1st Fd Amb, and who had also taken with him his own dental instruments, which were later augmented from Red Cross stores. Urgent medical treatment could also be arranged at the CCS, where a general duty sergeant, who was a dentist in civilian life, had obtained some equipment and did excellent work.

LOGISTICS: SUPPLY AND STORES

The medical services relied on others for adequate supplies of medical and surgical equipment, drugs and dressings. If these were not forthcoming, or this supply was interrupted, they were effectively neutralised, as improvisation had its limits. This is why the problem of stores and supply is important in understanding the activities of the AAMC at Anzac. There were big differences between the supply system as it operated in France and on Gallipoli.

At first everything – medical stores, even food – was scarce. Recalling the first few days after the landing, Corbin, commanding No. 1 ACCS, wrote that although tea and biscuits were plentiful, in the first days after landing that was all they had to eat. By the end of April there was a marked increase in the number of boats available for bringing in stores.

The situation did improve gradually, as this description by Beeston, commanding the 4th Fd Amb dug in at Anzac Cove, testifies. By May the beach was 'a mass of supplies of all kinds ... The rations are all of the best ... and the men are not stinted as to quantity. The biscuits though are very hard on the teeth'. One particular type of army biscuit was known as a 'forty-niner', as it had 'forty-nine holes in it, was believed to take forty-nine years to bake, and needed forty-nine chews to the bite'. The availability of such rations at Anzac, however, depended on how well the distribution system worked.

PROFITEERING

Quantity was not the only problem. Quality, particularly of Australian-made medical supplies, was often unsatisfactory, with Army standards being openly ignored, as this medical unit diary indicates:

> I draw your attention to the first field dressings issued to many of the men – made by Elliot Brothers Australia. There is no doubt that they are a disgrace & a definite menace as being grossly inefficient. I herewith send on in the condition as when opened. The rubber tissue is not sealed simply folded – dirt & dust penetrated the dressing.

To illustrate this point, an enquiry was held under the *War Precautions Act 1914-1916*, into the purchase of medical and surgical stores and pharmaceutical goods for the Australian forces. In one case the difference in the individual price of hypodermic syringes between two military suppliers was seven shillings and sixpence. Given that this was more than most soldiers' daily pay, the amount is significant. As this particular report stated, military standing orders for purchasing medical equipment had been almost entirely ignored - so much for selfless patriotism at home.

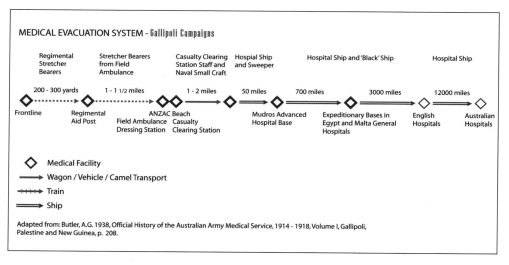

The problems in the area of supply of medical and other equipment were compounded because the responsibility for supply was shared between three organisations. The AAMC supplied and distributed drugs, dressings and instruments internally, while the Army Service Corps looked after food and 'medical comforts'. The Army Ordnance Department supplied stretchers, tents, beds, blankets and hospital equipment. There were other considerations, and the ubiquitous army red tape was a constant source of frustration for medical field units running out of vital supplies. A problem in any one of these organisations had direct repercussions for Australian units deployed on Gallipoli

A congested Anzac Beach looking south to No. 1 Australian Casualty Clearing Station within the first days of the landing at Anzac Cove. (AWM PS1488)

The AIF on Gallipoli depended on British supply units, which worked on a system under which each Army Corps had its own depot on the peninsula. The problem therefore was not always one of insufficient sources of supply, but rather finding enough small boats to transfer stores from ships to the peninsula. There were several British medical supply depots on both Lemnos and Gallipoli.

As we have seen, the drain on medical stores as a result of the unexpectedly heavy casualties resulting from the August Offensive was compounded by the increasing incidence of sickness at Anzac. The AAMC reported to the supply authorities that it was experiencing great difficulties in obtaining an adequate supply of medical comforts and drugs.

The shortage of farinaceous foods to combat diarrhoea was of major concern, and by August stocks were running dangerously low. Sutton, Howse's second-in-command, reported that the amount of arrowroot, cornflour and Bovril on hand for the 1st Division was sufficient only for one field ambulance for one day. There was no hope of combating diarrhoea and maintaining the strength of combatant units.

Despite its best efforts, the Australian Red Cross could supplement only to a small extent the huge demands made by the Diggers at Anzac and in Egypt. As the British Red Cross had the responsibility for all Red Cross work on the Lines of Communication, the Australian branch's activities were centred in Egypt. There were British Red Cross stores at Alexandria and, by May, at Mudros, which were eventually drawn on by the AAMC. The Australian Red Cross established a depot of its own on Lemnos in October.

An attempt was made to set up a Red Cross depot on Gallipoli 'but it was blown away on the first day it was erected'. As it was not practicable to maintain permanent Red Cross depots on the peninsula, a regular system of delivery from Mudros was organised. The stores were sent in charge of a responsible Red Cross representative who either stayed on the peninsula while the stores were being distributed, or handed them over to the medical officer in charge. These stores consisted of items as varied as blankets, lemons, chocolate, syringes and formaldehyde.

One of the most significant contributions to the Gallipoli effort by the Red Cross was the provision of a picket boat and two Red Cross motor launches and crews, which were used not only for distributing Red Cross stores, but also for transporting senior medical staff around Mudros Harbour to oversee transport and hospital carriers, previously a real logistics gap.

The British Red Cross was also able to support the medical transport system by providing for the priority needs of hospital ships proceeding with sick and wounded to Alexandria and Malta. One of the sore points between the Australian medical services and the Australian Red Cross was the lack of medical comforts such as pyjamas, supplied by that organisation, on those ships bringing thousands of wounded from Gallipoli to Australia.

One of the many effects of the haste with which the whole campaign was undertaken was the poor loading of the MEF's stores, of which medical supplies and equipment were only a part. Unsuccessful efforts were made to prevent the despatch of stores before they could be properly sorted out at the dockside. As one officer wrote tongue-in-cheek: 'It only remains to be said that, three months after the opening of the campaign, the medical stores arriving in Mudros from England were still being found at the bottom of the holds of the store-ships. However they were to reach the peninsula in time for the evacuation'.

In view of the difficulty of discharging stores quickly at Mudros, the British Transport Department strongly urged that transports be sent direct from Britain to Alexandria, where the stores could be landed, sorted, and forwarded in smaller vessels to Mudros as and when required. The Transport Department's suggestion was not adopted, however, mainly to avoid exposing cargoes to a double submarine risk. This proposed solution might not have worked in any case. The essence of the supply problem was the lack of adequate small seagoing craft. It was observed that the Principal Naval Transport Officer (PNTO) had 'at this disposal barely enough craft for the daily requirements of the Peninsula and islands'.

There were other, perhaps less obvious, dangers. A confidential report sent to the British prime minister from Gallipoli stated that: '[I] should mention that the... routes [transports] are to follow are laid down by the French naval Commander-in-Chief, and, in passing, I would suggest that collisions might be less frequent if different routes could be laid down for outward and homeward-bound vessels'.

Senior officers were equally critical of the handling of stores, especially at Lemnos. On his arrival at Mudros the Chief Engineer of the ANZAC (Brigadier-General Alain de Lotbiniere) found that some vessels had been in the harbour for up to four weeks without any attempt being made to unload them. Due to the way in which ships had been loaded, it was impossible to get at the goods required in their holds without unloading what was on top.

As there was no space on deck and no harbour facilities at that time, the difficulties can be appreciated. On one transport there were over 80 tonnes of fresh beef. The captain, who was not able to unload it at Anzac, and needed the cargo space, threw the beef overboard. For future engagements, de Lotbiniere recommended that civilian contractors should be employed instead of naval personnel.

Australian hospitals setting up on Lemnos found that even basic hospital equipment was often unavailable for several weeks. Sister Louise Young of No 3 AGH recounted her experience of the arrival at night of troops from Anzac in August 1915. The patients were placed on the ground 'with a tarpaulin and blanket under them, another over them and not a stitch of clothing on them after cutting off their uniform'. She went on to describe washing the men in bedpans before theatre, because these were the only containers holding water that could be procured or borrowed at that time.

Australia and the AAMC must share some of the blame for the shortfalls in medical and related stores during the campaign. The logistics system was further confused by uncertainty regarding Australia's responsibility for providing supplies at Anzac. This was complicated by the ambiguous and often uncoordinated role of voluntary supply organisations, particularly the Australian Red Cross. Auxiliary services, such as X-ray equipment and bacteriology laboratories, were also in very short supply. The situation in Egypt was little better.

THE HUMAN COST

After the heavy fighting in August, and with the very hot weather, limited variation in rations and high stress levels, an alarming increase in the already high incidence of sickness and disease was inevitable. Howse described an inspection he carried out of the 5th Battalion on 18 August, recommending that 'the men require a good long rest and unless they get it soon many of them will suffer permanent ill effects and be unfit for further active service for at least one year ...'

By 10 September the 2nd Australian Division arrived to reinforce the Anzac garrison, and small numbers of troops were taken to Lemnos for periods of one or two weeks for rest. Many were suffering from exhaustion, but were still keen to fight on. In an interesting comparison the *New Zealand Army Medical History* states that in the NZ&A Division alone, the average losses through sickness amounted to 100 per 1000 per week, while the rate for troops in France at the same time was five per 1000.

These were a sorely needed respite, and the Diggers could hardly believe their luck. Lieutenant T.W. Garling wrote that he and his men disembarked at Mudros Harbour at 1600, and after a march of over 30 kilometres they arrived at their rest camp on a hillside overlooking the harbour. 'An advance party had been sent on and they had tents erected and a jolly good feed waiting for us. We were dog tired and turned in immediately after tea … Duties are very light, the main object of the camp being to give the men a thorough rest.'

Commanders on the peninsula were insatiable in their demands for reinforcements. Once the casualty rate began to climb again during August, the repercussions for field commanders were brought home when expected replacements for men sent away to rest or recover failed to appear. This important aspect of the work of the AAMC, to restore fighting troops to the front as soon as they were well again, also highlights what at first appears to be a failure of the Australian medical services in 1915.

Although 'processing' the wounded was a vital role of the medical service, it was poorly understood by the general staff. During April and May Howse complained that 50 percent of the casualties leaving Anzac (suffering from slight wounds or illness) would, under normal circumstances have been returned to duty within three to four weeks.

At that time the weekly evacuation rate from Anzac was over 2000 men, few of whom were actually returning to Gallipoli. Howse considered it 'essential that urgent steps be immediately taken to return Officers and other ranks who are fit for duty … in fact it has become a byword at Anzac that, once evacuated, it is improbable that they will return for many months'.

Problems with transport, inept processing of paperwork, and lack of reliable shipping timetables, together with the relative ease with which some determined individuals could evade their duties, did not help matters. One illustration is provided by this signal on 5 May from Lieutenant-Colonel Alfred Bennett, commanding the 4th Battalion. It is quoted in full because it became a common complaint from all the infantry commanders on Gallipoli:

> I desire to bring to serious notice the disadvantages and inconvenience caused by lack of information concerning the whereabouts, condition, and probable period of absence of officers and men, who leave the battalion on account of wounds, sickness while on duty. It is only from hearsay and from returned officers and men, that information is gleaned and that cannot, of course, be relied on or acted on officially …

Even at No. 1 AGH in Cairo, convalescing patients were allowed to roam the city's streets at will for several months until the hospital's administrative procedures were tightened. On the other hand, conscientious Diggers complained that they were hampered by red tape when trying to make their way back to their units on the peninsula. Others didn't complain or could not cope, and sought to escape Gallipoli.

PSYCHOLOGICAL PROBLEMS: SOLDIERS AS HUMAN BEINGS

There were also less tangible problems that had to be dealt with by the medical services on Gallipoli. Although not as obvious as wounds and disease, nonetheless these became the responsibility of the medical service. Like its Imperial and dominion counterparts, and indeed the enemy, the AAMC was totally unprepared for this type of battle casualty, even though the numbers actually involved were relatively small, and certainly not on the same scale seen on the Western Front from 1916.

The understanding of the causes and management of mental illnesses in 1915 was primitive at best. Freud was still largely unknown outside his native Vienna. It was not a topic that had ever been taught in any European military medical service, and its treatment was still viewed with suspicion by the wider medical community.

'Shellshock', although a misnomer because its causes were not clearly understood, was first recognised during World War I, and men suffering from it on Anzac were not diagnosed as such for some time. Some shellshock was perhaps better classified as shell concussion, and was caused by being close to a bursting shell of high calibre. But, as one authority at the time wrote, 'in men already worn out or having previously suffered from the disorder, the final cause of the breakdown may be so slight, and its origin so gradual, that its origin hardly deserves the name of "shock" '.

Once it was recognised that direct physical trauma was not always involved, an Australian medical editorial stated: 'It is already very obvious that the war will bring us many cases of little understood nervous and mental afflictions, not only where a definite wound has been received, but in many cases where nothing of the sort appears.' Many such men continued to suffer well into the late 1930s and beyond, misunderstood by their families and distrusted by the authorities, their lives shortened or ruined beyond repair.

An instance was recorded by Sister May Tilton, who remembered nursing a 20-year-old:

> who regained his reason but lost his voice. This was attributed to shock. He told me in the faintest whisper that he saw his two elder brothers killed in one day on the Peninsula. He went mad and wanted to rush the 'Turks' trenches; remembered being prevented; then knew no more. He could not understand why he could not talk.

A less sympathetic medical officer, A.J. Campbell wrote that 'Without being malingerers, these men generally exaggerated their disability, and as carriers of psychic contagion were a source of danger in a ward, therefore we always endeavoured as far as possible to isolate them'.

The conditions of Gallipoli did not offer the same opportunities for the Diggers to relieve tension that were available to troops on the Western Front, in terms of rest, leave, recreational facilities, and military brothels. It was inevitable then, that for some soldiers something had to give. In its milder form this usually took the form of poor morale and then, increasingly, minor infringements of military discipline. This affected both combatant and medical units, as both experienced the same dangers and shared the same environment. During July several members of the 3rd Fd Amb, and in August several men of the 5th Fd Amb, were punished for insubordination and refusing duty.

Apart from Diggers presenting to medical units either sick or wounded, there were also accident victims, who added to the burden on the medical service. Some were quite serious, and missing hands or fingers from improvised grenades hitting the back of a trench before they were thrown were common.

There were also stupid incidents, such as one on board a troop ship, when a Digger was playing with his rifle, which discharged. The bullet went through the wall, blowing off the head of a sleeping soldier in the next cabin. In the absence of what is now practised as risk management, common sense was held to be the best protection. Of course, not all incidents were accidents. Self-inflicted wounds were also far from rare.

Not long into the campaign, the strain at Anzac became so great that men began to inflict wounds upon themselves in the hope of being evacuated. Typical examples are recorded in personal and war diaries. 'During the night nine self-inflicted wounded men were transferred to me from the 6th Fld Amb.' Even troops new to Anzac felt the strain. Sergeant Harry Woods of the 4th Fd Amb noted in his diary that a newly arrived man of the 16th Battalion 'purposely blew off his foot, and was detained in custody'.

The situation became so bad that as early as 26 May special instructions were issued with regard to the prevalence of self-inflicted wounds. These were repeated again in July, and each succeeding month. In June one hospital patient was 'to be sent back to Anzac when better to be tried for shooting himself through the hand'.

These incidents, understandable though many of them may be, are in stark contrast to the Anzac soldier of popular myth. The official historians rarely used this material to highlight the fragile state of some men under the conditions of battle stress.

Some medical officers viewed this type of behaviour very censoriously, and there are moral overtones in some of their letters and diary entries. Many other doctors were caught between their civilian experience, in which their role was that of a caring confidant, and their responsibility as officers who were being used to determine whether casualties were 'shirkers', or were really sick. It was a dilemma for some medical officers, and for many the most distasteful part of their military experience.

Unless life-threatening situations were involved, all cases of self-inflicted wounds were retained and treated in medical units on Anzac under the MEF's Standing Orders. The war diary for November of the 2nd Fd Amb notes: 'As many as half a dozen men were in the ambulance at one time with these injuries. They generally took the form of a bullet in the left hand or left foot.'

Even senior medical officers were aware of developments, and Porter wrote to his wife that he had heard 'disturbing tales of self-mutilation – blowing off fingers so they cannot shoot'. All such cases still had to be held and nursed by front-line medical units, units whose personnel would certainly have related to the same stressors. Other Diggers took less drastic measures to get an early ticket off Anzac and some resorted to eating explosive (cordite).

There were also occasions when medical personnel were less than enthusiastic in the front line. Captain A.Y. Fullerton, the RMO of the 2nd Battalion, wrote that before one battle he lined up his medics and the regimental stretcher-bearers behind their old trenches and warned them they would follow 'close on the heels of the last company of our Battalion (the 2nd)' with as many dressings and as much iodine as they could carry.

As soon as the last riflemen of his company had gone over the sandbags, Fullerton led his men forward, to find that he was accompanied only by his batman and two medics when he reached the enemy trenches! Later he 'rounded up the whole lot of the AMC unit and the regimental stretcher-bearers. The next day I told them I expected they would all be shot for cowardice …' Fullerton was perhaps unique, in that before this particular engagement the RMOs of the 1st Brigade had decided that they would not accompany their units, but would wait until dark before joining them.

Rheumatism, which became very prevalent in November in the cold and wet weather, was also used by a few as a ploy to escape Anzac. 'On a sunny morning a Medical Officer would get his rheumatic cases out into a dry creek bad and make them walk slowly up and down while he sat on the bank closely scrutinising them and trying to distinguish the malingerers from the genuine cases.'

Remaining at Anzac, whatever the cost, became a point of honour among many of the originals. The bonding of mateship, and therefore a mutually supportive social structure, was much stronger among the veterans than, for example, the untried units of the 2nd Division. All that newly arrived Diggers saw at Anzac was a stalemate. They had not taken part in the initial assault or any of the big attacks. For them Gallipoli was siege warfare, with its inevitable and soul-destroying drudgery.

CHAPTER 8:

An Assessment

The scale of the Gallipoli landing and the nature of the preparations undertaken are of prime importance to understanding the role of the AAMC. 'However easy it may be to draw attention to blunders made or problems left unconsidered – and insufficient preparations to attend to casualties is an obvious example – it should be recognized that the scale of the task was unprecedented.' We conclude this study by drawing together the threads of some important themes.

PROBLEMS AT THE APRIL LANDING

Well before the landing, the Imperial environment within which the AAMC was obliged to work was poorly prepared, and too inflexible to cope with this type of hastily executed operation. For Australia's part, the AAMC and most of its officers had a poor understanding of their responsibilities as military officers and doctors. This was to be expected, as most had come from an entirely civilian background, and like other officers in the AIF, they became better with time.

The Australian Government had a *laissez faire* attitude to its medical services. The Commonwealth also over estimated the capacity of an overworked British war machine to minister adequately to the needs of Australian wounded, and this had profound implications for the AAMC and its ability to operate effectively.

The magnitude and unprecedented nature of the initial phases of the Gallipoli campaign caused massive difficulties, particularly for medical services so manifestly subservient to other arms of the MEF. The uniqueness of the amphibious campaign (which was woefully ill-prepared, despite its complexity) was arguably too great a challenge at times for the untried Australian medical services.

Added to the deficiencies in numbers, experience and equipment, there was the necessary subordination of the AAMC to an Imperial machine that knew little of Australian ways. Individual events, taken together, also made a significant contribution to the medical debacle during the first days after 25 April. Important among these was the late arrival at Lemnos of the *Hindoo*, the absence of any overall medical controlling officer at Anzac Cove, and the radio communications blackout during the landing, and again in August. On a smaller scale there were other factors, such as inadequate physical screening of the volunteers for poor eyesight and other medical and dental problems, which later added to the medical workload and diluted the fighting strength of the AIF.

At the highest levels of the Australian Government there was a mistaken assumption that the provision of treatment, transport, and accommodation of wounded and sick troops would be undertaken by the War Office. This state of affairs was compounded by the lack of any subsequent delineation of the respective responsibilities of Australia and Great Britain. This applied particularly to hospital ships, but there are numerous other examples.

Bridges did not help matters by ignoring his senior medical advisor, Williams, before 25 April. Birdwood ordered his QMG to intervene in a desperate and well-meant attempt to clear the backlog of casualties after the landing, completely upsetting Birrell's medical evacuation plan.

Hamilton and his staff, by their decision to leave behind those staff members directly responsible for medical arrangements for the MEF, were guilty of poor management. This decision, together with secrecy and wild optimism surrounding the potential success of the landing, were responsible for many of the problems encountered in April by the Australian medical services on Gallipoli.

Unit training within the AAMC was interrupted in Egypt by outbreaks of sickness there, including VD, with which the medical services then had to cope. In addition, the usual British medical organisation for field service, under which the AAMC and the NZAMC operated, was based on land warfare. There was no extant doctrine for amphibious operations. As there was simply no space in which to deploy many elements such as tent subdivisions, medical units ran into trouble at the landing through lack of manpower and the rapid dissolution of rigid plans and military doctrine into irrelevance.

RELATIONS BETWEEN THE ARMY AND THE ROYAL NAVY

Babtie, the first officer to hold the appointment of PDMS for the Middle East, arrived in Egypt in June. His appointment was the result of an attempt by the War Office to resolve the medical problems that had occurred in April. The navy, for the same reason, appointed Porter as the PHTO. His arrival in Egypt on 24 July added to the confusion. Altham, the Inspector-General of Communications, wrote that:

> at the present moment, I find, on my return this afternoon from General Headquarters, concentrated here Surgeon-General Babtie, Surgeon Birrell, Colonel Maher, DDMS and Surgeon-General Sir James Porter. I have in fact to face the most extraordinary embarrassment of a superfluity of expert advisers the relations of whom with each other are exceptionally ill-defined and unsatisfactory.

This statement characterised relations between the military and naval medical authorities throughout the Gallipoli campaign. The strained relations between the two services are perhaps best illustrated by the role of Porter, a former Director-General of Naval Medical Services.

On 15 June 1915, at the request of the services, a conference was held at the War Office, which was to have implications for the Australian medical services on Gallipoli for the ensuing five months. The conference appointed Porter to be 'Principal Hospital Transport Officer to cooperate with Surgeon-General Babtie of the Dardanelles ...' with respect to the transport of the sick and wounded.

However, the British army's senior medical officer, Keogh, later admitted that the navy was unaware before the conference that Babtie had been in control of hospital ships in the Mediterranean since he arrived there three weeks earlier. The Admiralty would never have suggested Porter's appointment if Babtie's role had been understood. This is one of several instances of poor liaison between the services.

The objects of this June conference were to organise a regular service of hospital ships for severely wounded troops to work between the Dardanelles and Britain, and to arrange ferry services for lightly wounded cases between the Dardanelles and Alexandria, and the Dardanelles and Malta. A subsequent submission, sent to the First Sea Lord on 21 June, expanded Porter's role to ensure that there was combined utilisation of naval and military resources in respect of sea hospital transport in the Mediterranean, under the superintendence of a single authority to be known as the 'Hospital Transport Officer (Mediterranean)'.

By the time Porter received his instructions two weeks later, his brief had been expanded. The Admiralty then wanted him to inspect and report on the naval hospital ships *Rewa*, *Soudan* and *Somali*, and the provision made in them for embarking and disembarking, transport, and treatment of wounded generally. He was also to direct the movements of all sick and wounded of both services by sea in the Mediterranean.

The berthing and general movements of hospital ships would continue under De Robeck, but Porter was also to satisfy himself that the medical and nursing staff and the outfitting generally of all hospital ships were adequate for the work required. As it was the army, not the navy, which was responsible for supplying medical officers, nurses and orderlies to most of the hospital ships, the potential for conflict can be appreciated.

Hamilton was informed on 28 June that Porter was on his way, and was told that 'the Naval and Military Medical officers will inform [Porter] of their wants, and arrangements will be made by him for sea conveyance on hospital ships, subject to the usual control of the Senior Naval Officer'.

Up to this time Babtie had been in charge of hospital ship movements. Hamilton was quick to realise what such duplication of effort would mean, and the next day cabled to London:

> I hope you realise that this creates one more link of possible friction which I will try to avert to the best of my powers. Babtie has just arrived and is a most capable man. He does not know anything yet of the new appointment. He has worked out a scheme of evacuation of sick and wounded by land and sea. Who is to be 'boss'?

When Porter visited Babtie in Egypt on 21 July, both he and Ford (DMS Egypt) denied any knowledge of his official appointment, and even Maxwell, the GOC in Cairo, knew nothing at all of Porter's appointment as PHTO. At least Hamilton seems to have been giving some thought to future complications, for on 3 July he cabled the War Office, and asked that the respective responsibilities of Porter and Birrell be clearly defined.

On 28 July, Porter arrived at Mudros and reported to both De Robeck and Hamilton. Porter complicated matters further by setting up his own separate headquarters, not at Imbros on the flagship, or with the DMS, MEF, at GHQ, or at Lemnos with the Inspector-General of

Communications and the PNTO, but on a small yacht, the *Liberty*. There, though personally mobile, he was without wireless communications, and was unable to respond promptly to rapid changes in the situation as they arose.

To summarise to this stage, a naval surgeon was appointed over an army doctor to take charge of a medical evacuation scheme designed entirely along vague lines by the army, using the resources of the navy. Neither medical arm of the two services had worked with the other on such a scale before. Added to this was the failure of the War Office to notify all senior officers of Porter's appointment, an omission that heightened personal animosities among the participants.

Despite Porter's approach to the general staff at this time, he could obtain little information concerning proposed operations, apart from the intimation that there was going to be a 'push' made at Gallipoli on 6 August. Porter managed to obtain a plan of the operations to ascertain what arrangements had been made for the wounded, reviewed them, and decided they were grossly inadequate in terms of the necessary hospital ships.

After the war Maher (who was ADMS Mudros on board the *Aragon*) wrote that Babtie's scheme added to that of Birrell by placing hospital ships as near the beaches as possible, and sending them down the lines in what Babtie 'called a ferry service, i.e. a vessel or vessels leaving whether full or not and plied to a time table to Egypt and Malta'. In consultation with the new DQMG, MEF, Ellison, Porter modified the original plan and arranged for eight hospital ships to lie off Gallipoli when the August Offensive began.

The two main stumbling blocks during the five months that Porter was PHTO were first, duplication of control; and second, the demarcation of army and naval responsibilities 'at the high water mark' on the beaches. This opinion was echoed in a variety of sources. On 26 September 1915, a letter from Field Marshal Lord Methuen (Governor of Malta) to the DGAMS illustrated the difficulties inherent in the system for hospital ship transport in the Mediterranean. He also condemned dual control by Porter and army authorities.

These stumbling blocks would continue to plague medical arrangements at Gallipoli until the end of the campaign. Even before Porter's appointment was terminated in November, certain medical officers, jealous of their own prerogatives and professional standing, failed to cooperate fully with him. This, together with Porter's own shortcomings, further hindered the efficient medical evacuation of Australian casualties from Gallipoli.

Porter noted that complaints had been made of the inadequate number of medical staff on transport ships, together with the state of these ships. However, these areas were wholly army, rather than naval, responsibilities. He 'recommended that the appointment of Hospital Transport Officer should be abolished'. This would again make Babtie responsible for evacuation and distribution of casualties.

In response De Robeck sent a letter to the Second Sea Lord on 3 October 1915, arguing that before Porter's appointment the situation had been one of chaos, where the RAMC was lending assistance. De Robeck believed that attempts to have Porter withdrawn emanated from Babtie, 'a person whose sphere of interference could with advantage be curtailed'; and whom he thought was anxious to have Porter's yacht *Liberty*. He concluded by requesting that the Second Sea-Lord 'do anything to retain Porter'.

Moves began at the Admiralty to call an enquiry, because of suspicions that Porter had not received the loyal support of the army's senior medical officers. Later, on 19 November 1915, the War Office informed the Admiralty that as a result of the experience of the past three months it recommended 'that … the normal system of control of hospital ships should be reverted to and that the responsibilities of Surgeon-General Sir James Porter, in the matter, should cease at as early a date as possible'. In part this was a realisation that the dual system did not work, nor could it against the complexities of the overall Dardanelles campaign.

At a general level, relations between the army and the navy reflected the situation that existed between Porter and his military contemporaries. (This is not to suggest that a state of perpetual antipathy existed between all members or units of the two services.)

Even before Porter arrived at the Dardanelles, one of De Robeck's aides (Wemyss) wrote that the military medical arrangements were entirely inadequate, and that Birrell was absolutely incompetent to deal with the situation. Wemyss admitted to almost coming to blows with Birrell because he refused Wemyss' offers of assistance by sending naval surgeons on board transport ships sorely in need of medical staff. He also wrote of 'the fact of the General Staff refusing to go on shore and detaching themselves from everybody and everything …'

The navy was the first to realise what the army was only then coming to terms with, that the conditions of Gallipoli, unprecedented as they were, demanded a different approach to handling medical matters, and medical evacuations in particular. The old methods were no longer valid, at least in this campaign.

Under the new system, the Admiralty would make separate arrangements for the sick and wounded of the Fleet. Those naval hospital ships and naval medical staff which had been on loan to the Army would again be placed under De Robeck's control as Senior Naval Officer, and would be allocated for purely naval purposes. These problems of communication and cooperation in the medical services were not restricted to the high command of the army and the RN.

ANZAC AND BRITISH RELATIONS

There were times during the Gallipoli campaign where relations between the AAMC and the RAMC were less than cordial. Fortunately, such occasions did not have lasting or important consequences for the proper functioning of the medical services'. The Australians themselves were often responsible; at other times the Imperial authorities were the source of friction.

At the beginning of 1915 the AAMC, AIF was intended to be absorbed wholly into the MEF, and essentially to become an Imperial organisation. Australian authorities were to be responsible for the raising, outfitting and training of Australian medical units, but the plan was that once these personnel reached the base in Egypt, they would immediately come under the direct control of the British PDMS, Babtie. However, British senior medical officers had assumed for their part that the internal administration of the AAMC units under their control would be the continued responsibility of Australian officers.

In Egypt especially, a number of Australian medical units were under the direct supervision of RAMC officers, which caused a great deal of animosity and valid criticisms from the Australian medical services, such as this comment by an Australian doctor: 'It is hard being under R.A.M.C. men who though quite nice know not the officers nor the organisation and constitution and don't try very hard to find out'. In a letter to Fetherston, Brudenell White wrote that the:

> cost to Australia of medical arrangements in Egypt is enormous. All that cost is at present being incurred by RAMC Officers who are not responsible for their action to the Australian Government … From the Australian point of view this alone makes provision of some effective administrative machinery, a necessity.

The Australian military authorities contributed to the confusion by not supporting their own DMS, Williams, when he arrived in Egypt early in 1915. Fetherston also was convinced it would have been much better if the Defence Department in Melbourne had initially taken the position that in Australian matters the AAMC would do things in its own way, and insisted on having its wishes carried out. However, the Australian Government seemed content to throw in its resources unconditionally to the Imperial cause.

Williams' British counterpart in Egypt, Ford, had only just been appointed as chief medical officer for the British commander there, Maxwell. The Australian commander, for his part, did nothing to support Williams. Some of the rivalry stemmed from misunderstandings brought about by men and women coming from very different backgrounds.

There were reports of Australians in British field hospitals having insufficient to eat, not enough blankets, and not having their wounds dressed. No doubt some of these reports were based on hearsay. There were also Australian troops who spoke highly of British hospitals, and standards in both British and Australian run hospitals varied as to staff, supplies, and facilities, as they do today.

Charles Ryan, an experienced army surgeon, remembered working with the British. 'My experience on board the *Soudan* was the reverse of pleasant through the unwillingness of the Consulting Surgeon to co-operate with me'. The most bitter comments came from Australian field officers such as Captain A.G. Carne, the RMO of the 6th Battalion: 'When we worked and fought side by side with the British troops at C. Helles the British stretcher bearers refused to assist our men, collecting only their own wounded, passing by Australians; while our men attended to British and Australian alike'. An entry in the war diary of the 3rd LH Fd Amb noted that the officer in charge of stretcher-bearers of the British 39th Fd Amb had refused a request for help from his unemployed stretcher-bearers.

Some were critical of the lack of professionalism of senior British medical officers. Babtie eventually arrived on Gallipoli to see the situation for himself. His inspections, at least at Anzac, were rather short. According to Corbin of No. 1 ACCS, Babtie was at Anzac Cove for two and a half minutes, while Corbin did not see Porter at all on Anzac.

Howse was very critical of Birrell, but added that he 'considered he was ill, when I saw him, and I did not think he was physically fit to grapple with such a big situation as existed, which required a good deal of initiative'. The reason is no doubt that Howse was a very strong personality with strong views. It is not widely known that he threatened to resign over the question of dual Australian and British control of the AAMC. He wrote to the DGMS, stating that he would 'be glad to be relieved of my duties at the earliest possible moment unless the Minister of Defence is able to support my view'. At the end of 1915 he got his wish.

While Babtie was not an organiser of any great calibre, his colleague Birrell was found out first, possibly because of Hamilton's dislike of him. Hamilton wrote in September that 'he does not in my opinion possess the exceptionally brilliant qualities desirable in the medical chief'. However, not all relations were antagonistic, indeed had they been the Gallipoli campaign would have been an impossibility. There were many instances of close cooperation between various medical units of the different armies.

The British were well aware of the defects in the Australian organisation. Writing of the April landing at Gallipoli, Hamilton said: 'True, owing to accidents, inexperience, shell fire and defective organisation of the higher medical authority in the Anzac Corps, there was a partial breakdown of the Australian section of the scheme during a few days'. This observation was correct, as the Australians experienced problems with their senior medical administration at the time of the April landing. This was due both to the organisational deficiencies mentioned above, and to the refusal of either Howse or Manders to take on the responsibilities of DMS, ANZAC.

Birrell could see the obvious defects in the Australian arrangements at Gallipoli, and there is little doubt that senior officers of the AAMC were to blame for some of these inadequacies. Two years later Birrell wrote to Hamilton that there had been no trouble with casualty evacuations further south at Cape Helles, which were carried out under the same conditions, but there the ADMS of Division remained with the HQ. Birrell continued that 'if the two ADMS at Anzac had done the same and not landed to do the work of junior officers on the beaches the confusion Surgeon General Howse states occurred at the landing would have been avoided'.

However, criticisms of the British have to be tempered by an analysis of the frictions within the different Australian medical units and among medical personnel serving throughout the Gallipoli campaign. The latter were chiefly medical officers, as most of the trouble emanated from professional jealousies brought intact from Australia.

INTRA-AUSTRALIAN RELATIONS

As early as May frustrations building up within the AAMC were becoming known far afield. The Governor-General, in a letter to King George V, wrote that the 'medical service both here and in Egypt has been disappointing. In Egypt, [this is] largely because of the friction between medical men, all of whom being great swells in the profession find military discipline irksome …'

Relations between individuals and units within the AAMC were not immune to the organisational and personal weaknesses that have been discussed above. Fetherston 'quickly found that there was considerable confusion in the Corps, and discontent among all ranks in the AAMC'. One of his staff officers believed that most of this trouble in Egypt (which reflected the larger situation) was due to the fact that there was no Australian authority responsible for the administration of its own medical units, and for the treatment of Australian casualties from Anzac.

Complaints included quarters, seniority, and promotions. Unfortunately such strife was not confined to those directly involved. In September 1915 the Governor-General wrote to Maxwell that the 'Medical Department seems to give by far the most trouble ... These doctors...are singularly destitute of any sense of discipline'. This strife sometimes spilled over into the public arena:

> There has been considerable controversy in the Public Press over the English administration of the Red X supplies ... extraordinary acerbity developed amongst Australian Doctors at the Front. There are eminent Surgeons among them, but personal rivalries and mutual antipathies destroyed their sense of decency and discipline ... Probably it will take a series of libel actions to calm some of them down!!

Brudenell White wrote to Fetherston in September that he particularly wished to speak with him about the medical arrangements for the Diggers, as the 'present position is by no means satisfactory'. He did not blame individuals, but 'the lack of organisation'. Apart from interstate jealousies that arrived with the 1st AIF convoy, there were also complaints about promotions and seniority with in the AAMC, especially by those officers on Gallipoli.

Such were the politics and personal rivalries that bedevilled the medico-military operations on Gallipoli and in the rear. These factors together asserted undue influence on what ultimately was done for the sick and wounded on Anzac. Subsequently, the relative success of the treatment and evacuation of Australians is almost remarkable, given such obstacles.

A ROYAL COMMISSION

In August 1916 the British government appointed the Dardanelles Commission to investigate, among other issues, glaring inefficiencies and bungling in the treatment of wounded during the Gallipoli campaign. It published two reports, one in 1917 and a second in 1918, and its deliberations make interesting reading. The Commission highlighted cases of infighting, and blatant attempts by British staff officers to pass the responsibility for mistakes to others, or even to refuse to recognise the very existence of serious errors and shortcomings in their own departments.

Throughout the proceedings of the Commission different witnesses in the medical and other departments complained of two problems. The first was Hamilton's decision in March 1915 to leave behind his administrative staff in Alexandria, and the second was Hamilton's personal remoteness and inaccessibility.

The second complaint concerns senior officers being denied access to Hamilton, mainly through the intervention of his Chief of Staff, Major-General W. Braithwaite. This complaint was supported by Woodward, who earlier had suggested to Hamilton that the landings be postponed for two days so that medical arrangements could be placed on a proper footing. Braithwaite may have blocked (deliberately or otherwise) Woodward's request to Hamilton.

Woodward stated that he saw Braithwaite on the eve of the landings to point out that the medical arrangements were inadequate. He suggested that the operations should be postponed until he could make more definite arrangements. Woodward insisted on seeing Hamilton personally, because he thought there would be trouble about the wounded, but Braithwaite refused to cooperate with him.

Braithwaite later denied this, but from the available evidence he may have been a key figure in the decision not to postpone the landings at Anzac and Cape Helles until the medical arrangements were complete. Braithwaite's obstruction could have been intended to shield Hamilton from the more minor worries of a large and complex campaign. In any case, this approach had serious consequences for the Australian medical services, and especially those Australian doctors who tried, *via* Birdwood or Godley, to have Hamilton correct deficiencies.

Australian army witnesses called before the Commission did not mince their words. Howse responded to a question in this way:

> I think the outcry, both in Australia and amongst our own men – not only in the medical Corps has led to a great deal of feeling against the Imperial authorities. I have heard officers of some rank … say they consider it was murder, and … would lead them to report to their Government that under no conceivable circumstances would they advise the Commonwealth of Australia to enter again upon any war where they were entirely placed under the authority of the British Headquarters.

During proceedings Corbin stated that there were no major improvements in medical arrangements after April, and the state of affairs was as bad in the operations in August, mainly because there was no means of clearing the beach. However, he did concede some improvement, as in his later testimony that 'we had nothing like the same amount of surgical work in proportion to the number of cases to do. In addition to this, there was infinitely better and more ample hospital ship accommodation [than in April], and so many cases who would have died under other circumstances were rushed on to the hospital ship for operation'.

An experienced AAMC officer, Ryan, in his evidence before the Commission stated: 'I should think there must have been thirty of these large transports lying there. They were simply empty ships, not in any way suitable for a hospital … In some of the ships there was a fair staff of medical officers; in others very few. There were no nurses at all, and we had no modern conveniences for surgical operations.'

Views, for or against, were invariably strongly expressed when the Gallipoli campaign was discussed, either in general or in its the medical aspects. A New Zealand doctor (Major Purchas) when giving evidence before the Commission said: 'I should say the medical arrangements for the Dardanelles business was about as puerile as anything ever was'.

Despite all the evidence to the contrary, Ford, when asked whether he was at any time short of hospital accommodation, vehemently denied it. 'No. I think in Egypt we were rather ahead of events, because we built up the anticipation of a large number of wounded – we did not know how many because unfortunately there was no interchange of opinion between the M.E.F. and the Headquarters in Egypt.'

The fact that the French were better supported throughout the campaign calls into question many of the excuses put forward at the time to explain why the AIF could not be similarly supplied, particularly with water, vegetables and fresh bread. Stories of poor provisioning, the non-appearance of foodstuffs from Australia, and the lack of canteen facilities, with the increase in sickness among Australian troops, gave rise to much criticism in Australia.

Eventually pressure began to be exerted through official channels. Late in August Hamilton received a telegram from Kitchener, in which Hamilton was asked to report about rations generally, their variety, and whether canteen stores sent in July and August had been received. He was also asked to explain 'the cause of debility of such an excessive number of men among the Australians'. By this time other organisations, notably the YMCA, the Australian Comforts' Fund, and to a lesser extent, the Australian Red Cross, had started to establish themselves, and they provided material support to the casualties and other patients of the AAMC.

In September Howse disputed official British reports, which stated that supplies of rations to Australian troops were adequate. He cited a number of supply returns that indicated severe inadequacies in the supply of fresh bread, vegetables and frozen meat. He also refuted a further criticism, which stemmed from a British supply depot, concerning the assumption that the abnormal amount of jam and molasses consumed by Australian must have contributed to the increase of diarrhoea. 'As no molasses has been issued to the 1st Aust. Div. it cannot have been a factor and I do not believe that well made jam could account for such a type of Dysenteric Diarrhoea that exists at Anzac.'

The DAG for the MEF, Woodward, was later questioned on this point by the Commission. One of its members told him that Birrell had stated that casualties' rations were supplemented by lighter foods such as arrowroot, rice, tapioca, condensed milk; and that rations could be changed to rice or oatmeal from bully beef and biscuit. Woodward's reply was that vast supplies had been sent to Anzac, and more medical comforts than to any other part of the occupying force. In other words, he claimed that the Australians had the best of everything.

When questioned before the Commission, Godley stated that it was entirely possible that his men were unaware of the opportunity for substituting other foods for bully beef and biscuit, due to his Division's QMG staff not publishing the fact in routine orders to commanding officers and company officers. Godley also agreed that this amounted to a neglect of duty on the part of his QMG staff.

The following comment typifies, rightly or wrongly, the view held by a number of medical officers at Gallipoli, including senior British doctors: 'except for the presence of hospital ships I do not consider the methods of evacuating have improved one iota since the time we landed here, 25 April, 1915 …'

Andrew Fisher, the former Australian prime minister, who replaced Sir George Reid as High Commissioner in London in 1916, wrote a memorandum concerning Gallipoli, admittedly with the benefit of hindsight. As the Australian High Commissioner in London, he was a member of the Commission. Fisher believed that the 'initial provision of men, equipment, transport, medical services, and of intelligent proportion for contingencies was inadequate – a fault that was never fully rectified'. As for the arrangements for wounded, there were 'unheard of hardships, unnecessary suffering by uncomplaining men ...' Fisher was highly and unjustly critical of Porter, but rightly censorious concerning the luxuries enjoyed by staff officers aboard HMS *Aragon*.

The *Final Report* of the Dardanelles Commission stated: 'The scheme for the evacuation of the wounded in the August operations was based upon an approximately correct estimate of casualties, and the supply of hospital ships was much larger than at the first landing. On the whole, this scheme worked well, though again there were cases in which the improvised hospital ships were not satisfactory' and the wounded suffered – again.

The preparations made by the AAMC, although adequate for dealing with operations in the Anzac sector, were seriously upset by the relatively large number of casualties and by the lack of communication (and insufficient notice) from Hamilton's GHQ.

SOME CONTEMPORARY VIEWS OF THE MEDICAL WAR

What at first sight might appear to be a peripheral subject does have an important bearing on the history of the AAMC at Gallipoli. It concerns the opinions of the part played by the Australian medical services in that theatre. These included those of war correspondents, editors, and the combatants themselves.

The AAMC had sufficient problems with which to cope without receiving criticism from Australia. This is not to suggest that the Australian press withheld praise where it was due, but the organisation of the medical services was often subject to criticism (unfair or otherwise), whereas on other occasions timely observations and reporting by the press may have assisted the AAMC and its morale.

In March and April 1915, while loose tongues in Cairo ensured that anyone who cared to listen knew that there would soon be an offensive on Gallipoli, little in the way of accurate information found its way to the Australian government. Despite this, the government remained totally committed to Britain's war aims, and was not diverted from its support to the mother country. From May 1915 the records of Australian parliamentary proceedings rarely indicate any debate over the medical situation in Gallipoli itself or the treatment of wounded. The uncensored letters of soldiers, medical and nursing personnel had to filter back before people in Australia began to understand just how grave the situation was.

Fetherston, the acting DGMS in Australia, went to Egypt and the Dardanelles on a fact-finding mission. His report to the Australian Secretary of Defence was for the most part accurate in its assessments, and certainly the more abysmal shortcomings were identified, as were basic administrative shortcomings within the AAMC itself.

Fetherston noted that in addition to the naval medical command, AAMC units had to work with separate military authorities in Egypt, Britain and the MEF. These three groups were distinct commands, independent of each other, and each with its own general officer commanding.

Fetherston also identified one of the underlying causes of medical mismanagement. He levelled severe criticism at senior British medical officers who 'were given positions for which they were not suited'. More importantly, he pointed out that the dissatisfaction, disorganisation, and wasteful expenditure which occurred at places like Mudros could only be solved by sending out soldiers who were also businessmen and able administrators, for war, with its many hospitals and other medical units, was now being run like 'a large business concern'.

This was an evolution in thinking, particularly at senior command level, reflecting as it did the complexity of modern warfare. The medical services were ill-suited to conducting the integrated administrative and fiscal functions carried out today by specialised health bureaucracies.

In private, senior British medical personnel and Australian officials who were aware of the problems besetting both the RAMC and the AAMC often wrote of their concerns to superiors and colleagues. Bedford, one of the abler senior British doctors during the Gallipoli campaign, wrote to Keogh at the War Office in September 1915: 'I must say that I am very concerned with the wastage from sickness which is going on … Unfortunately the figures are gradually rising and the week ending 18/9/15 represents an annual wastage of 240.7 percent of troops; this is from disease alone, and does not include any casualties from wounds'.

Bedford was also thoroughly pessimistic concerning the longer term at Gallipoli. He had spent the previous day at Anzac where he found 'a good deal of sickness … It was rather a surprise for me to find this condition of affairs … I fear we shall be faced with great difficulties if we have any prolonged spell of bad weather'.

Fisher pointed out that the 'initial provision of men, equipment, transport, medical services, and of intelligent proportion for contingencies [was] inadequate – a fault that was never fully rectified'. As for the arrangements for wounded, there were 'unheard of hardships, unnecessary suffering by uncomplaining men …' The New Zealand High Commissioner, Sir Thomas MacKenzie was more forthright: 'Until August 1915 the arrangements for dealing with the transport of wounded were a very unsatisfactory state, and, indeed, the medical side of the campaign does not seem to have every been thoroughly thought out'.

Despite some apparent jealousies between the British and Indian Army Medical Services, the AAMC had few complaints about its allies on the peninsula. Lieutenant-Colonel H.W. Bryant, commanding No. 1 ASH, was most grateful for help provided by the French in lending him mule carts, drivers and mules to shift eight tonnes of medical equipment and stores. He noted that the Australians were 'greatly indebted to the French for their assistance and courtesy on all occasions as required it'.

There was no negative criticism of the other actors in this drama, namely the Indians, the Ghurkhas or the 500 strong Zion Mule Corps, which consisted of Russian Jewish volunteers who had fled Palestine at the outbreak of war, and subsequently arrived in Egypt. The Canadians, who operated hospital facilities on Lemnos, also appear not to have roused the antipathy of their Commonwealth colleagues.

THE PRESS

For the most part the Australian press relied on syndicated correspondents such as Charles Bean, Ellis Ashmead-Bartlett, Philip Schuler, and a handful of special correspondents working from Alexandria and Cairo.

The London *Times* was critical of the Dardanelles campaign throughout 1915, and described the experiences of the wounded at the April landings as 'one of the most discreditable phases of our participation in the war'. The *Times* blamed the lack of cooperation between the Admiralty and the War Office.

However the Australian press were surprisingly moderate in their coverage of the medical problems *per se*, and the actual mistakes of the Gallipoli campaign. Interestingly, the Australian press rarely reported on the medical aspects of Gallipoli, except for the occasional feature like the Treatment of Wounded that the Melbourne *Age* ran. It is less understandable that those papers which maintained their own correspondents for various periods at the front could only reprint features from the *Times*, although the censor doubtless played a part.

The often frank commentaries and opinions in private diaries kept by army officers were not translated into public statements. Curiously, however, a number of private letters suggesting there were serious problems at the front were not only allowed back to Australia, but were published there. The Melbourne *Argus* occasionally published letters that had been written from medical personnel to their relatives. At no time did these allegations lead to any special comment, further articles, or enquiries by this paper.

Between May 1915 and January 1916 only one editorial relevant to the AAMC was printed by the *Argus* (on 2 September), and it concerned Fetherston's voyage of inspection 'at very considerable cost' to Egypt. The question of whether Australian wounded were adequately looked after in Britain was also addressed periodically. On 23 October 1915, the *Argus* reported that the 'New South Wales Agent-General [Mr B. Wise] has informed the Commonwealth High Commissioner [Reid] that he has received well-founded complaints as to the neglect of wounded soldiers in England, which suggests that there is insufficient organisation to deal with the wounded'.

However, there were no articles on the evacuation of wounded troops from Gallipoli, nor anything to suggest that there were, or had been, serious medical problems. The only hint of trouble came in a few lines in the *Argus* of 6 November 1915, which related that complaints had been made public in New Zealand concerning the poor quality of bully beef and its contribution to sickness on Gallipoli.

By contrast the Melbourne *Age*, publishing material from its special correspondent Schuler (and others), gives a different perspective on the AAMC and the problems it faced. Schuler devoted rather more time to the medical services. In contrast to the *Argus*, from October 1915 the *Age* published a series of potentially damning articles concerning medical conditions, in which the problem of the shortage of small craft was identified.

Then, on 15 October 1915, it published a further piece from Schuler, who thought that it was 'time to sound a note of protest against the medical organisation, or rather the lack of it, and the treatment of the wounded … The blame, if any, rests more on Imperial than Australian shoulders …'

The article went on to say that a lack of organisation, foresight and supervision were the main reasons for the breakdown in the medical arrangements. It identified two parts of the problem: conveying wounded men from the beaches to the bases, and the arrangements for the reception and treatment of the men at the bases. 'General Birrell was in command of the first branch, and General Ford, as director of medical services in Egypt, the second'.

Under the headline Treatment of Wounded – Sheeting Home the Blame, the *Age* special correspondent on 18 October 1915 wrote of the inadequacies of the system by which Red Cross stores were being distributed both in Egypt and on board hospital and transport ships. This was not so much an AAMC problem, but a Red Cross affair.

A number of related articles appeared in the *Age* during the remainder of October. Schuler pleaded that he had not spoken out earlier, and had 'suppressed any hint of the sufferings of the troops' because he wanted to spare a public regularly in receipt of casualty lists additional suffering. Interestingly, the *Argus* made no such report during the same time, in spite of Ashmead-Bartlett's increasingly critical reports to the British newspapers, which were being reprinted in the Australian press.

The *Sydney Morning Herald*, relying on the same sources for its news, reported those issues covered by the *Argus* and the *Age*. However, a number of soldiers' letters were published in which the transport of wounded from Gallipoli was vividly described. Again the theme was that all was well. The paper stated that 'although nothing official has been announced by the Defence Department with regard to the progress made by the Australian wounded … the injured men are doing well …' It later published a statement made by a British official denying that arrangements for the reception of wounded at Alexandria were inadequate.

The reproduction of some private correspondence from wounded Australians by this paper is curious, as some of these related to the appalling situation aboard the *Seang Choon*. Throughout July the *Sydney Morning Herald* published a series of private letters, often written by AAMC personnel at Anzac or in Egypt, which were extremely critical of medical arrangements and the conditions under which the Australian medical services had to work, but they were unaccompanied by any editorial comment. No letters from readers were published, nor were there any editorial comments on statements by politicians.

The Sydney *Bulletin* was silent on the issue of Australian wounded at Gallipoli and their subsequent medical treatment. Its editorials appear to have been heavily influenced by The *Times* editorials, and its publication of Hamilton's complete despatches in the preceding month. The *Bulletin* concluded that the 'Generalship of the landing at Gallipoli failed to complete the work of the soldiery. In August it did the same thing, with more painful consequences'.

FINALLY

In some respects the costly lessons of April had been learned by August; in others it was obvious that not everything had been heeded from the original landing. As we have seen, throughout the Dardanelles action Australia had no real control over the larger medical policies that so often affected her troops.

In August the Australian medical services were better prepared than many British units, despite inadequacies in areas beyond Australian control. Whereas in April the stretcher-bearer subdivisions of the field ambulances had been retained on board ships until the confusion of the landing had been sorted out, this was not a problem in August.

At a higher administrative level, Babtie's preparations were substantially incomplete by the time of the August Offensive, with some medical reinforcements not arriving at Mudros until 7 August, and even then with equipment missing or lost. Porter's contributions have been mentioned, and these must have helped avoid a repeat of the disastrous April events. Despite his other shortcomings, Babtie had organised an expansion of hospital accommodation on Lemnos. Many of the same administrative and tactical errors of April were repeated in August, and these adversely affected medical operations.

AIF wounded and sick were at once both beneficiaries and victims of British policies. The War Office supplied and controlled the means of evacuation, directed the location and staffing of the base hospitals, provided supplies of drugs and medical equipment for a large part of 1915, and above all established the infrastructure in which the AAMC performed as a small and subordinate player.

Australia should have insisted that in Australian matters it would do things in its own way, with AAMC officers in charge. Had the Australians followed the Canadian example and demanded autonomy for their medical units, the situation may have been altogether different. The problems this caused during the April landings were still not entirely resolved by August, and an administrative solution was not found until early 1916.

Disease and sickness, absent in April, also had an impact in August, when some front-line medical units were under strength. Conversely, finding medical personnel to care for casualties on transport ships was a major problem in April. This was less so in August, due to more comprehensive planning and medical reinforcements along the Lines of Communication. The dental issue was beginning to be addressed, and the fitness of reinforcements arriving from Australia was more rigorously assessed, both on Gallipoli and in Egypt. This eased the pressure on the AAMC at the front, on Lemnos, and in Egypt.

To summarise, despite better planning the August Offensive suffered some of the same shortcomings seen in April. There were insufficient hospital ships and small boats, a lack of effective communications, and a shortage of stretchers.

In August, however, there were more personnel in some areas (particularly as all subdivisions of field ambulances were utilised), there was better and more comprehensive planning, accurate maps were made available, and there were more stores available. Sufficient officers had at last been nominated both to sort casualties and to direct them to shore or ship, and this was a definite improvement. There was also a keen appreciation of the implications of large numbers of casualties for medical units such as stationary and general hospitals along the Lines of Communication.

The problems faced by the medical services during the Gallipoli campaign were exacerbated by personal animosities and professional jealousies. Relationships between individuals and units within the AAMC were not immune to professional and personal weaknesses, and complaints about quarters, seniority, and promotions. These strains impaired the efficiency of medical units from Gallipoli to Cairo.

Undoubtedly the AAMC was subject to the same mistakes in judgement and the same human weaknesses as every other wartime organisation. Too often in the past an uncritical eye has scanned the activities of the various medical services of the AIF and cast them as the unwitting (but always innocent) prey of a heartless and rigidly bureaucratic Imperial juggernaut.

This study has sought to show that the Australian Government and the Defence Department made serious mistakes. Most of these were founded either on a naive faith in the ability of Great Britain to provide resources in abundance, or the disinclination of some senior AIF commanders to heed advice.

For their part, the British military authorities must answer for the lack of adequate arrangements to coordinate Lines of Communications units, which caused the deaths of many surgical cases. The AIF has to accept responsibility for a number of 'casualties', particularly dental cases. Poor screening of men at Australian recruit depots, 'cheating' by over-eager volunteers, and laxity on the part of civilian doctors employed for medical inspections, were all sources of later medical trouble on Gallipoli.

The selflessness and highly visible bravery and dedication displayed by the AAMC on the peninsula, and along the Lines of Communication, hold an important place in the later folklore surrounding the Anzacs. At the initial landing and throughout the subsequent campaign, there is no doubt that individual doctors, medics, orderlies and bearers acquitted themselves admirably. There were doubtless many AAMC members who would have been eligible for the Victoria Cross, but history has not recorded their exploits, which were often carried out alone and out of sight, or cut short by shell or shot.

The periods from the end of May until the August Offensive, and the months from September until December 1915, constituted lulls in heavy and large-scale fighting. Even in the absence of large numbers of battle casualties, however, a depleted AAMC was kept busy. Many of the original medical units, in common with their fighting colleagues, were exhausted.

With the hot weather came disease and sickness, mainly dysentery, diarrhoea and enteric fever. The policy of retaining men at the front worked against the standard health practice of isolating disease carriers, so re-infection was almost guaranteed. In several field ambulances holding facilities were set up where sick, as opposed to wounded, men could have a few days' break on 'soft' rations. The onset of disease exacerbated the shortages of medical manpower at the front, and caused a backlog of sick men in the field ambulances and smaller medical units at Anzac.

The largely unsuccessful battle against the fly continued during this time. This period also coincided with an acute shortage of water, and inadequacies in the supply and variety of rations. The daily routine continued with delousing, sick parades, and preparation for winter. This meant laying in stores, consolidation of old dugouts, and other medical housekeeping chores, and sanitation.

A highlight was the arrival of the 2nd Division in August. Subsequently the 1st and 2nd Fd Ambs were relieved by the 6th, while the 4th Fd Amb went to Lemnos after being relieved by the 7th. Overall, this was a time for consolidation and battling against disease, both tasks which fully occupied the medical services, particularly those AAMC units at the front.

With regard to Hamilton's generalship, some commentators maintain that a 'picture of unrelieved incompetence by Hamilton and his staff at every level cannot be maintained'. But Colonel (later General Sir) Brudenell White observed of Hamilton that his concern for (or perhaps his understanding of) the Lines of Communication 'appears to have been in the slightest. He took everything for granted, and took but the slightest concern in the arrangements for preventing the emasculation of his Force by unnecessary losses through sickness and wounds'. Hamilton's immediate staff shared this attitude. This is not to suggest total indifference, but at that time it was not popularly recognised by general staff officers how valuable a part the auxiliary branches play in a complex allied operation in modern warfare.

The bronzed stoic Anzac is still a strong popular icon in Australia. Few texts point out that they suffered the same psychological and disciplinary problems as other troops serving in the MEF. J. Murray was one of a number of British authors who published their own experiences of these phenomena. One of his colleagues put his thumb over the muzzle of his rifle and pulled the trigger; Murray had to cut the remnants off with a marlinspike.

Episodes of disobedience, shirking of responsibility, cowardice, self-mutilation, fear, jealousies and dishonesty did occur, all traits that extended to members of the medical services. There were cases of medical officers beating a hasty retreat to the safety of Cairo's hospitals. While these are observations, not judgements, they still should be part of our understanding of what it is we celebrate on 25 April.

The Australian AMS received its baptism of fire on Gallipoli, which moulded it into the efficient organisation of 1916. The stage on Gallipoli was set by Great Britain, which supplied the major actors, while a relatively small role was accorded to Australia, whose military skills evolved under the shadow of its larger ally.

The constant, unrelieved strain of trench warfare, together with unvaried diet, the daily routine, wounds and illness, took their toll on many Diggers. The face of Captain Henry Fry of the 10th Light Horse Regiment shows the strain. He was killed on 29 August in a bayonet charge on the Turkish trenches on Hill 60. (AWM A05401)

In the few areas in which they had autonomy, the Australian medical services also reflected some of the contradictions of efficiency and pettiness that characterised several senior British officers in the MEF. Under the resolute leadership of capable officers, however, together with a growing appreciation of the independence of their Corps, these problems were grappled with and largely solved by the time the Gallipoli campaign drew to a close.

Out of the brutal tragedy of Anzac a tradition of medical care and organisation was born, one that began to utilise many uniquely Australian qualities. Australia's medical services left the shores of Gallipoli sobered by their experiences, having served friend and foe without fear or favour. But this was only the first of many conflicts for which they would have to prepare, suffer, and survive in the service of Australia and humanity.

Some Statistics

COSTS OF THE CAMPAIGN

The physical sufferings and mental anguish of the men and their families and friends cannot, of course, be measured. Non-fatal casualties, as a proportion of the strength of the AIF during the Gallipoli Campaign (May to December 1915) were:

DATE	EFFECTIVES	TOTAL SICK and WOUNDED	PERCENT
1.5.15	21,066	4021	19.08
1.6.15	24,334	5126	21.06
1.7.15	25,498	4606	18.06
1.8.15	29,067	6255	21.52
1.9.15	21,814	7134	32.70
1.10.15	27,843*	7960	28.59
1.11.15	30,451	7317	24.03
1.12.15	27,035	7285	26.95
1.1.16	33,540	8213	24.48

* The first reinforcements began to arrive at this time.

AIF AND NEW ZEALAND DEATHS FROM ENEMY ACTION ON GALLIPOLI:

	Killed in Action	Died of Wounds	Wounded	Total
AIF	5833	1985	19,441	27,259
AAMC	33	35	225	293
NZ	1904	495	4852	7251

OTTOMAN CASUALTIES ON GALLIPOLI:

Hospitalised sick: 354,634   Hospitalised wounded: 343,648

Died of Disease: 44,407   Died of Wounds: 7756

Combat deaths: 56,127

While they were consistently outnumbered by the allies, Ottoman and allied losses were approximately the same. It is estimated that 115 Ottoman army medical officers died in 1915, mostly from typhus. The French lost a staggering 47,000 men of the 75,000 they sent to the campaign.

ESTIMATED POPULATIONS IN 1914:

Australia: 4,940,000

Great Britain: 45,000,000

France: 39,000,000

New Zealand: 1,100,000

Germany: 65,000,000

Ottoman Empire: 22,000,000 (of which Ethnic Turks: 12,000,000)

Financially, the total cost of the Gallipoli campaign to Australia (which was to be reimbursed by Britain) was assessed at £2,416,428. To provide some meaningful comparisons, the consolidated revenue of the Commonwealth of Australia in 1913-14 was £21,741,755, while its entire Defence expenditure in that year was £1,547,921.

An idea of the scale of medical support supplied to the MEF can be gauged from the following statistics. In the Dardanelles theatre itself, seven general hospitals (1040 beds each), five stationary hospitals (400 beds each), eight casualty clearing stations, and 15 field ambulances had to be kept fully equipped with trained personnel, medical and surgical stores and equipment, food and water. Stores provided included 4.5 million bandages, 5972 kilometres of gauze, 340 tonnes of lint and wool and 186,000 shell dressings.

Selected Bibliography

PRIMARY SOURCES

Australian War Memorial, Canberra - A.G. Butler Papers, AWM 41; Dardanelles Commission Proceedings and Reports, AWM104; Fetherston Papers, AWM2 2DRL 1200.

National Maritime Museum Greenwich London - Papers of Admiral Sir James Porter PRT/8/, Papers of Admiral Sir Arthur Limpus, Ms75/139.

Liddell Hart Centre for Military Archives, London – Papers of Sir Ian Hamilton (various)

PUBLISHED WORKS

Bean, Charles, *The Story of Anzac*, vol 1, 1924, rpt, University of Queensland Press, Brisbane, 1981.

Butler, Arthur, *Official History of the Australian Army Medical Services*, Vol 1, Australian War Memorial, Melbourne, 1930.

Official History of the Australian Army Medical Services, Vol III, Australian War Memorial, Canberra, 1943.

Carberry, Arthur, *The New Zealand Medical Services in the Great War 1914-1918*, Whitcombe & Tombs, Auckland, 1924.

Dardanelles Commission, Final Report, HMSO, London, 1919.

Erickson, Edward, *Gallipoli: the Ottoman Campaign*, Pen & Sword, Barnsley, 2010.

Ordered to die: a history of the Ottoman Army in the First World War, Greenwood, Westport, 2001.

Hikmet Özdemir, *The Ottoman army, 1914-1918: disease and death on the battlefield*, University of Utah, Salt Lake City, 2008.

McPherson, William and Thomas J Mitchell (Eds.), *History of the Great War, Medical Services General History*, Vol IV, HMSO, London, 1924.

Prior, Robin, *Gallipoli: the End of the Myth*, UNSW Press, Sydney, 2009.

Pugsley, Christopher, *Gallipoli: The New Zealand Story*, Hodder & Stoughton, Auckland, 1984.

Robertson, John, *Anzac and Empire*, Hamlyn, Melbourne, 1990.

Travers, Tim, *Gallipoli 1915*, Tempus, Stroud, 2001.

Tyquin, Michael, *Little by Little: a Centenary History of the Royal Australian Army Medical Corps*, Australian Military History Publications, Sydney, 2006.

Tyquin, Michael, *Madness and the Military*, Australian Military History Publications, Sydney, 2008.

Yalman, Emin, *Turkey in the World War*, Yale University Press, 1930.

Index